Gentleman
AMATEURS

An Appreciation of
Wilbur and Orville Wright

By Mark Bernstein

Photo Research by Marvin Christian • Edited by Ron Rollins • Designed by Sol Smith

Produced by

Dayton Daily News

Published by
Dayton Daily News
45 South Ludlow Street
Dayton, Ohio 45402

Printed in the United States of America

First printing 2002

ISBN 0-9656649-4-5

Acknowledgements

The producers of this book wish to thank the following people and organizations, without whom the project would not have been possible.

▶ Special Collections and Archives, Wright State University Libraries, particularly Dawne Dewey, John Sanford and Jane Wildermuth.

▶ The *Dayton Daily News* Reference Library, particularly Martha Hild.

▶ Imaging specialists: Lou Lucchetta, Steve Adams, Scott Allen, Mary Lair and Beau Wyatt.

▶ Book team photo on dust jacket: Skip Peterson.

▶ Co-workers who enabled this project: Brad Tillson, Mark Stange, Jeff Bruce, Steve Sidlo, Mike Ausra, Jane A. Black, Vicki Denney, Sherry Heinzerling, Lou Lucchetta, Amy Rollins, James Tyler, Jana Collier, Bob Underwood and Ken Canfield.

▶ Family support: Irmgard Christian, Amy Rollins and Deborah McCarty Smith.

Contents

Gentleman AMATEURS

An Appreciation of

Wilbur and Orville Wright

Introduction

The Wright brothers are well-heard-of, rather than well-known. Common knowledge of Orville and Wilbur does not much extend beyond the facts that they were from Dayton, built bicycles and conquered flight. What is lacking is not the incidental knowledge that Orville voted Republican but talked socialist, just to annoy his sister-in-law, or that Wilbur had but one known social date with a woman – which is to say, one more than Orville. What is lacking is an appreciation of their natures and of the nature of their achievement.

The Wrights are not well understood personally. Often, they are cast as a type – a couple of Ohio boys with mechanical aptitude, grit and a general Midwestern shortage of personality. More accurately, they were "gentleman amateurs," who launched into flight out of a curiosity for the thing itself, out of Wilbur's desire to do something large with the life he felt was slipping away and Orville's desire to do something interesting, and with Wilbur. Launched, they had no immediate intention beyond solving the problem. They wished to determine if flight was possible. Even after the pair had flown at Kitty Hawk, they could imagine no larger use for their invention than that they might make demonstration flights at county fairs.

The Wrights are underestimated in their abilities. They were "passionately precise people" who brought to the task of flight no formal training but, as events were to prove, all the needed skills: Skill as designers, skill as carpenters, skill at mathematics, skill in photography and, most, skills of intellect and temperament – the capacity to conceptualize large, to master details, to hang with the problem, to face down discouragement.

They are underestimated in their achievement, the single most impressive piece of individual research and application in the 20th century. The Wrights accomplished the whole of the task, solving by turns the central problems of lift, control and thrust. Their work holds up: Their systems for getting airborne and for maintaining control while airborne are the only ones in common use.

The Wrights suffer most from retroactive inevitability, the view that because flight was achieved, it was therefore inevitable, and pending. In 1900, H.G. Wells – whose *War of the Worlds* described intergalactic combat – wrote that humans might actually fly "probably before 1950." In December 1901, Admiral George W. Melville stated, "Where, even to this hour, are we to look for the germ of a successful flying machine?" On October 22, 1903, the astronomer Simon Newcomb asked how any machine that flew could ever land safely. The year Wells wrote, the Wrights tested their first glider at Kitty Hawk, North Carolina. The month Melville spoke, they conducted their wind-tunnel experiments. The morning after Newcomb's views were published, the brothers began attaching their craft's landing skids.

Eight weeks later, Orville and Wilbur and several assisting lifeguards moved the Wright Flyer into position on the treeless sands at Kitty Hawk. And the damn thing flew.

▶ Above: Orville and Wilbur Wright in France, 1909.

He had a cyclist's body and a cyclist's stamina.

Orville

When Orville Wright was a child, he collected bits of tar from the side of the road, rolled the bits in sugar, wrapped them in waxed paper and sold them to friends as chewing gum. Orville, then as later, went his own way. On the fourth day of kindergarten, Orville dropped out of school, a move he did not report to his mother. He continued to leave each morning and to arrive back home each noon, on schedule. His mornings, however, were spent not in class but playing at the home of a friend, with one eye on the clock. Susan Wright did not learn of his truancy until she came to school two weeks later to see how her son was faring. Unruffled, Orville returned to class.

As an adult, Orville was fastidious, almost a dandy. Each year when the Wrights returned from their aeronautical pursuits at Kitty Hawk, Orville sponged his face with lemon juice to draw the Carolina sun out of his skin. He was sweet, and sweet-toothed, putting four teaspoons of sugar in his tea. Sweet, but not soft. During the brothers' bicycle phase, Orville took up competitive racing and won a series of medals. He had a cyclist's body and a cyclist's stamina.

His humor was occasional, but edged. Returning once from a speech given by a candidate for state office, he reported, "If that man is honest, he should sue his face for slander." His mind, likewise, was quick; he was excitable, likely to jump from thing to thing. He was, most strongly, timid – he avoided association outside the family, particularly with women. After his mother's death, his sister Katharine became the maternal energy in his life. His life's companion, in many ways, was Wilbur.

▶ Above: Orville in 1878.
▶ Opposite: In 1903.

'Wright has that peculiar glint of genius in his eye...'

Wilbur

W̲ilbur could be a scold. He was the son of a bishop, and when he was the eldest living at home, he served as head of household during his father's frequent travels on church business. He was his mother's primary nurse while she was two years dying from tuberculosis. For Orville, work tended to be a form of play; for Wilbur, play often became a form of work.

In 1888, Orville used a home-built press to launch himself into the printing business. The enterprise gave him an excuse for skipping out on his senior year of high school. Orville did odd job printing and published a skinny newspaper, *The West Side News*, a juvenile sheet of jokes and sketches.

When Wilbur moved in, things formalized. The *News* became a "real" paper; the brothers expanded the weekly into *The Evening Item*, a full-sized newspaper with international, national and local news, including this remarkable report of life in Indiana: "Baseball is on the decline in Vincennes since the craze for chasing soaped pigs began." The paper circulated in Dayton, west of the Great Miami River that bisected town.

Daily journalism was work, not well rewarded. The Wrights tired of it. Wilbur editorialized in aggrieved tones: While more affluent entrepreneurs might be able to back a newspaper until it prospered, "we have only a small capital and do not care to wait a year before we begin to receive reasonable profits. It takes the people over here too long to make up their minds to support their institutions."

Contrasted with Orville, Wilbur was older, taller, darker, self-confident, a fine public speaker, broadly self-educated and, by various testimonies, "hawklike" in appearance. He caught the eye. In 1907, an Englishman meeting him at the railway station immediately picked Wilbur from the throng, then wrote a friend, "Either I am a Sherlock Holmes or Wright has that peculiar glint of genius in his eye which left no doubt in my mind as to who he was."

▶ Above: Wilbur in 1878.
▶ Opposite: In 1909.

Poised and ready

The Kitty Hawk life-saving crew – along with dogs and children – turned out to help with flight attempts in December 1903. The airplane is lined up on the track and ready to go as the crew waits for instructions from Wilbur and Orville. It was December 14, and the first successful powered flight would follow three days later.

I

Family and Friends

'I asked her to go to Oregon with me.'

The Bishop and His Lady

Milton Wright – later Bishop Wright – began a diary on January 1, 1857, and maintained it for 60 years. An entry in June 1857 brought the first appearance of that diary's second most important figure. Milton Wright wrote, "Had my first private talk with Susan Koerner." Milton and Susan had met at Hartsville College, a tiny religious school in Indiana. The talk to which Milton's diary referred was part religion, part romance. Milton was soon to sail via Panama to Oregon to undertake two years of church work. To his diary Milton confided, "I asked her to go to Oregon with me." Susan Koerner declined.

The two became engaged during Milton's absence. During his return trip, Milton spoke to a fellow passenger, then recorded in his diary, "He was a married man, and I was going to my bride." Milton and Susan were married two weeks after Milton's return, in November 1859. She would bear him seven children – five of whom survived and twins who died in early infancy. For years thereafter, Milton each year noted in the diary the twins' death days.

With Milton often gone on church business, Susan Wright was a strong influence on her children. From their mother Wilbur and Orville acquired two signal traits: their shyness and their mechanical aptitude. If there was something to be repaired in the household, or a toy to be made or mended, the task fell to Susan Wright. Bishop Wright was a butterfingers.

In the mid-1880s Susan contracted tuberculosis, which is a slow death. Hers came on July 4, 1889. Wilbur was 22; Orville, 18. Milton wrote in his diary, "And thus went out the life of my home."

▶ Previous page: September 1899 saw this gathering at 7 Hawthorn Street. Orville is standing.
▶ Above: Bishop Milton Wright.
▶ Opposite: Susan and Milton Wright.

Breaking bread

Pictured at a family picnic (L-R): Orville, Katharine, Milton Wright Jr., William Jenkins, Jim Jenkins, Horace 'Bus' Wright, Lottie Andrews, Lorin Wright and Netta Wright. The teakettle was kept warm on the car's running board.

Katharine Wright, by contrast, seemed pretty solid.

Their Only Sister

In 1899, Daytonians observing Orville and Wilbur flying their kites – flying kites, incidentally, while dressed in suits – inclined to the view that the brothers were a bit nuts. Katharine Wright, by contrast, seemed pretty solid.

Wilbur and Orville's sister had graduated from Oberlin, the country's first, and possibly best, co-educational college. She taught Latin at Dayton's Central High, at a time when study of the subject was still considered a good way to build character. As a teacher of Latin, Orville noted, Katharine had "the satisfaction of failing some of Dayton's most illustrious citizens."

Katharine's father, the Bishop, thought she had too much temper, but "a fine constitution." In photographs she appears both humored and reserved. In the Wright home, Katharine did not much cook or clean, but she did manage the household, largely relieving her father and brothers of such concern. She had no interest in mechanical things, considered her brothers' mechanic, Charlie Taylor, intolerably common – and for these and other reasons avoided the bike shop.

By the standards of the day, she was a successful woman. She was not, however, much impressed with those standards. It was her ambition to teach Greek – but, as she complained to a friend, the teaching of Greek was a privilege reserved for those with an appendage she lacked. Occasionally, she protested. In 1914, she helped organize a march through Dayton in support of women's suffrage. That march drew 1,300 people to the city's streets, including Orville and the Bishop.

▶ Above: Katharine's school photo.
▶ Opposite: With Wilbur, about to take off in Pau, France, 1909. It was Katharine's first flight, and her skirts are tied for purposes of both aerodynamics and modesty.

Putting on quite the show

In February and March 1909, Katharine accompanied Wilbur and Orville to Pau, France. Wilbur was training Count Charles de Lambert, Paul Tissandier and Capt. Paul Lucas-Girardville to fly. Shown (L-R): French flier Louis Bleriot, Tissandier, Lucas-Girardville, Wilbur, Mrs. Hart O. Berg, de Lambert and Katharine. Mrs. Berg was the first woman to fly.

▶ Above: Lorin (left) stayed near home and eventually became Wilbur and Orville's business manager. Reuchlin (right) made his life in Kansas.
▶ Opposite: Reuchlin and Lorin Wright.

Neither Reuchlin nor Lorin pushed.

The 'Unknown' Brothers

Wilbur and Orville Wright are among the best known of names. Many are aware of Katharine, their sister. But few have heard of the two older Wright brothers, Reuchlin and Lorin. Whatever quality prompted Wilbur and Orville to soar was not apparent in their older siblings. In his younger, unsettled years, Wilbur wrote to a relative: "I entirely agree that the boys of the Wright family are lacking in determination and push."

Neither Reuchlin nor Lorin pushed. Reuchlin regarded himself as an outcast. He once refused part of a family bequest, apparently in the belief that he was not as good a family member as the others and therefore less deserving. Some fly the nest; Reuchlin fled. He left Dayton for Kansas, intending to farm. Farming proved difficult, and Reuchlin took a clerk's position with the Kansas City, Fort Scot and Memphis Railroad, a post both small and secure.

Lorin began work as a bookkeeper for Farmers Friend Manufacturing in Dayton; eventually, he became his brothers' business manager. At one point Lorin, over-reaching, gave his occupation as "inventor" – a title to which he had some claim. Years earlier, Lorin was granted U.S. Patent No. 369,149 for his invention of improvements in a particular style of baling press. Lorin had a wife, four children and in 1913 purchased "a fine home" at Grand and Grafton avenues in Dayton. It is difficult to imagine what Orville thought of this; Wilbur, always incomplete, may have regarded Lorin's settled domesticity with some envy.

Solid citizens, and proud

A West Dayton reception committee was formed to welcome Wilbur and Orville back from Europe in 1909. The group posed with the brothers and their family in the back yard of the Wright house. The group included (L-R, standing): William Andrews, Frank Hamburger, William Kuhns, Lorin Wright, W.C. Reeder, Wilbur Wright, Webb Landis, Milton Wright, Albert Shearer, Lon Shank, Orville Wright, E.H Sines, Charles Taylor, (first name unknown) Hotchkiss, (first name unknown) McCullough and Bob Kelly. Kneeling are (left) William Kirchner, (right) Joe Boyd, Billy Landis and Ed Ellis.

The neighborhood was largely working-class.

7 Hawthorn Street

An interviewer once suggested to Orville that he and Wilbur had grown up without special advantage. Orville immediately disagreed. They had, he replied, been "lucky enough to grow up in a home environment where there was always much encouragement to children to pursue intellectual interests; to investigate whatever aroused curiosity."

The home, in truth, was physically a modest one, a two-story frame house at 7 Hawthorn Street. Milton and Susan Wright bought the home from its builder for $1,800 in 1870, when they moved to Dayton from Indiana. The family remained for 44 years, well beyond the time that the father's position or the brothers' fame could have provided something better.

When the Wright family moved in, the neighborhood was largely working-class. It was also new, extending along a streetcar line that ran west from downtown. The house, originally narrow and deep, was made more graceful by the addition of a porch across the front and down one side. Downstairs, the right-hand side contained kitchen and dining room. These were the domain of Carrie Grumbach, who cooked and kept house for the Wrights for several decades. The left side included the sitting room in which, in 1903, Orville cut and Wilbur sewed the "Pride of the West" muslin used to cover their first airplane's wings.

► Above: The sitting room was where Wilbur and Orville cut and sewed muslin for airplane wing coverings.
► Opposite: The Wright house at 7 Hawthorn Street.

The street they knew best

A quiet day on Hawthorn Street in 1910. The Wright house is second from the right, with the front porch.

▶ Above: Paul Laurence Dunbar hoped to become a lawyer or a journalist.
▶ Opposite: Dunbar, about 1900.

‘For the sake of heaven and the race, stop saying and go to doing.’

Paul Laurence Dunbar, Poet

O rville Wright skipped out on his senior year of high school, in 1889-90. A second Dayton youth excelled in his. Paul Laurence Dunbar was Central High's class poet, editor of the newspaper and president of the debate society.

Dunbar hoped for a career in law or journalism. After high school, he learned that no local employer would give a black man white-collar work. He had, he said, two options: He could be a menial, or he could be a poet. He choose the latter.

He published hundreds of poems, dozens of short stories, novels and other works. The era in which he wrote was a time of rising racism in America; Dunbar's best work faced into that intolerant storm. He wrote, he said, "to sing songs of God and nature, to prove to the many the few were human." Dunbar was tubercular, a condition he treated with raw onions and alcohol – which led to or intensified the alcoholism that hastened his death, at age 33, in 1906.

Dunbar's poetry is remembered, which is just. Unjustly forgotten are his essays. These offer insight, anger and edge, all seemingly modern. The first such essay appeared on December 13, 1890, in the inaugural issue of the *Dayton Tatler*, which was edited for Dayton's black community by an 18-year-old Paul Laurence Dunbar and produced in the Wrights' print shop by a 19-year-old Orville Wright. The paper made its debut, Dunbar wrote, "demanding the recognition that is its right." Addressing the 5,000 blacks then living in Dayton, Dunbar wrote:

> *The time has come when you should act your opinions out.... Bear in mind that the agitation of deeds is tenfold more effectual than the agitation of words. For your own sakes, for the sake of heaven and the race, stop saying and go to doing.*

Orville said of the *Dayton Tatler*, "We published it as long as our financial resources permitted, which was not very long." Three issues, in fact. It is difficult to know just how deep was the friendship between Paul Laurence Dunbar and Orville Wright. Orville, generally, did not have close friends. He and Paul knew each other when they were young and gifted and believed the world was their oyster, before one of them learned that oysters were white.

Classmates

Paul Laurence
Dunbar (back row,
left) in a Central
High School class
photo with Orville
Wright (back row,
fourth from
the left).

Wilbur's Limited Social Life

W ilbur Wright was a lifelong bachelor who joined but a single social club, one founded in the Wright family living room on October 9, 1886. That evening, the three eldest Wright sons – Reuchlin and Lorin and Wilbur – and seven other young men from Dayton's west side met to organize the Annual Club of the Ten Dayton Boys.

For the next half-century, surviving club members met each October to dine and compare notes on life. Mild men mostly, though with pretensions to untrammeled malehood: Their first dinner featured fried oysters, stewed oysters, raw oysters and iced Adams ale. Two were salesmen. One was a photographer. Another a bookkeeper. A machinist and a printer. Wilbur, 19 when he joined, gave his occupation as "Clerk, J. J. Hoffman's Grocery."

Except for Wilbur, they were of modest ambition. Except for Wilbur, they married. For them, big news might be the birth of a child; for Wilbur it was usually a change in occupation. One October, when the dinner was co-ed, others brought their wives or sweethearts; Wilbur brought his sister, Katharine. She, the minutes say, "told some amusing stories of college days" at Oberlin.

When a member announced wedding plans, the others took out dinged horns and trombones and played a brief requiem to his bachelorhood. By 1893, Wilbur was the only bachelor, a state which in the club's minutes he suggested might be permanent: "There is so little prospect of an increase in my family that the fox horns, trombones, dingbats, etc., which the club formerly kept for case of emergency are rusted, covered with dust." Wilbur added that he had once again changed vocations: He was now in the bicycle business.

► Opposite: Wilbur, about 1897.
► Above: The Ten Dayton Boys reunited in 1909. The event was captured in postcard form, and included (L-R): Joe Boyd, Wilbur Landis, Reuchlin Wright, Lorin Wright, Wilbur Wright, Frank Gilbert, William Andrews, Ed Ellis and Charles Olinger. The tenth member had withdrawn years previously.

Unchanged by fame

Wilbur's 1908 flights near Le Mans, France, made him
world famous. The French turned Wilbur's hat into a fashion
trend, but could not draw him into Parisian social life.
Wilbur preferred to spend his time alone, working on the
equipment. His hat, coat and bicycle are in this hangar.

▶ Top (L-R): John Patterson, Charles Kettering and James Cox.
▶ Above: Third and Main streets in Dayton, about 1900.
▶ Opposite: The Dayton post office building, about 1900.

Inventiveness was Dayton's leading export.

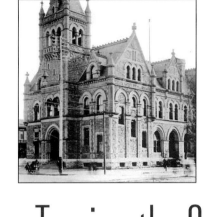

Dayton, Turning the Century

At one time, the U.S. Patent Office rated cities, counting the number of patents granted to a town's residents relative to its size. Measured that way, Dayton, Ohio, was in 1880 the nation's third most productive source of new patents. By 1900, it was first. With the new century, inventiveness was Dayton's leading export.

Followed closely by idiosyncrasy. Much of either stemmed from a spry, combative, intermittently vengeful man named John H. Patterson. As founder of the National Cash Register Company, he made his product the essential tool of retailing. He made his methods essential, too. He invented the trained sales force, sales territories, quotas and annual conventions, direct-mail advertising and the flipchart. Patterson liked a good feud. At one point, irked with local press coverage, he organized bonfires at which the publisher of the *Dayton Daily News*, James Cox, was burned in effigy. Cox, unsinged, went on to three terms as Ohio governor, founded a media empire and in the 1920 presidential election finished a distant second to fellow Ohioan (and newspaper publisher) Warren G. Harding.

Patterson had quirks – he took four baths a day and wore underwear stitched from pool-table felt; he fired inventor Charles Kettering six times and Thomas Watson once. Both took umbrage. Watson created IBM; Kettering left for the auto industry, where the electric "self-starter" ignition system he invented opened the door to mass acceptance of the automobile.

With cash registers, Dayton was showing the country how to sell. With the self-starter, how to drive. Wilbur and Orville would show it how to fly.

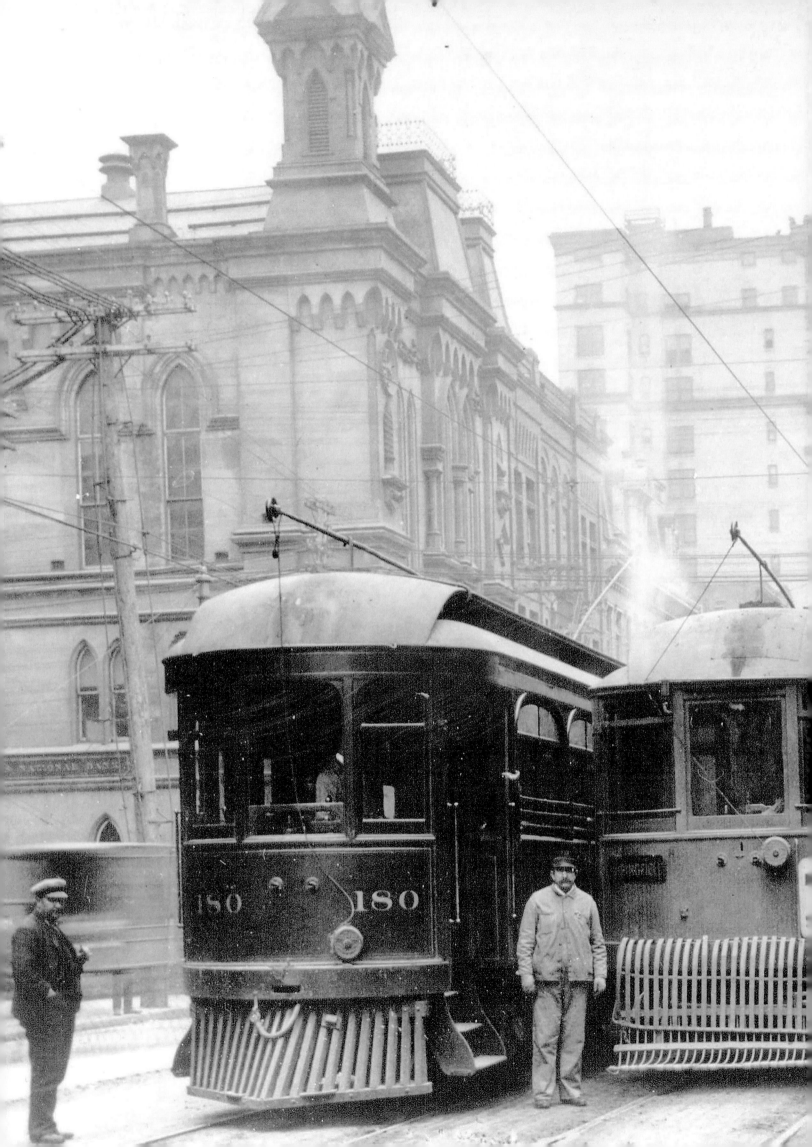

Clang-clang, clip-clop

In 1880, Dayton was, according to the U.S. Patent Office, the nation's third most productive source of new patents. By 1900, it was first. This late-1890s view looks west on East Third Street at Jefferson Street.

Landmark theater

The Victoria Theatre stood at the southeast corner of Dayton's Main and First streets in the early 20th century, and is still there.

AND CLASS ROOMS

PAINTS
WALL PAPER

PAINTS
WALL PAPER

WALL PAPER
WINDOW SHADES

PAINTS
Painters Supplies

130 THE SOL. RAUH & SONS C

WHOLESALE LIQUOR DEA

Where Dayton went to play

The Lakeside amusement park was a popular summer gathering place in Dayton. Opened in 1890, it was located west of downtown and offered bands, rides and other entertainment.

Heart of the city

Looking north along Dayton's Main Street from Sixth Street, about 1905.

Winter blanket

The center of downtown Dayton was – and still is – the intersection of Third and Main streets. The Old Courthouse, with its columned front portico, remains the major landmark, and stands on the northwest corner.

A brimming cornucopia

Downtown Dayton's popular, glass-domed shopping mecca, the Arcade, is shown here about 1910. The two-building structure opened in 1902.

2

Groundwork

A stick smashed Wilbur in the mouth, knocking out a number of teeth.

A Simple Twist of Fate

W hen Wilbur was 18, his parents expected that he would go to college. His older brothers, Reuchlin and Lorin, had each briefly attended Hartsville College, the small Indiana religious school where Milton and Susan Wright had met. Wilbur was to go to Yale.

One winter day he was skating on a pond near some kids who were playing a game akin to ice hockey. A stick flew out of one boy's hand and smashed Wilbur in the mouth, knocking out a number of teeth. Several weeks later, "nervous palpitations" set in. Wilbur was for months an invalid.

As a consequence, one almost never sees photographs of Wilbur smiling: he was self-conscious about the false teeth he acquired with the accident. There was a second, broader consequence. His uncertain health, his parents concluded, ruled out his leaving for college that fall. Yale was out; likely, whatever future Wilbur would make would be made in Dayton.

▶ Previous page: Orville (right) and Ed Sines busy in the Wright bicycle shop.
▶ Above: Wilbur attended Dayton's Central High School part-time in 1884-85.
▶ Opposite: Wilbur rarely smiled. He is pictured here in 1909 at a formal portrait session.

Playing on the ice

The frozen Great Miami River,
near Dayton's Main Street bridge,
was a recreational center in 1899.

Flight would be achieved by a cyclist.

Bicycles Built by Two

In September 1892, Wilbur wrote to Katharine about a 25-mile bike trip he and Orville made to Miamisburg, a riverside village south of Dayton. Their ride came in the midst of America's bicycle craze, sparked when the safety bike replaced the high-wheeler. In 1890, Americans bought 40,000 cycles; in 1895, 1.2 million.

Today's riders would rate these cycles as heavy, slow and expensive – Orville's 1892 Columbia cost $160, at a time when an average income was $12 a week. But the 1890s regarded them as light and remarkably quick. The bicycle was the first new form of personal transportation since the horse arrived in the Eocene, and bikes were easier to tame and to steer.

The Wrights were hobby cyclists. In 1893, they converted their hobby into a business, opening a bike shop on West Third Street. There, they sold and serviced bikes, then began building their own – the Van Cleve and lower-cost St. Clair models, named after local founding fathers.

Technically, bicycles were a bridge to the automobile. Bicycle production posed problems in metalworking, power transmission, tires and steering whose answers offered lessons for the motorcar.

Metaphorically, bicycles were a bridge to aviation. In 1896, the editor of the *Aeronautical Annual* hazarded that flight would be achieved by a cyclist. After all, he wrote, "To learn to wheel (cycle) one must learn to balance. To learn to fly one must learn to balance." Cycling itself was perceived as a form of flight. As early as 1882, *The Wheelman* said of the typical cyclist, "All men who ever walked have wished that they might fly; and here is a man who can hitch wings to his feet."

Wilbur shared the association. In his letter to Katharine he wrote, "Just as we came into Miamisburg we coasted a hill fully a half mile long and steep – whew! We came down a-flying."

▶ Above: The back of the Wright Cycle Company at 1127 West Third Street in Dayton.
▶ Opposite: To promote their bicycle business, the Wrights published *Snap-Shots of Current Events*, a weekly publication geared to cyclists.

Corporate headquarters

The front of the brothers' West Third Street bike shop, about 1910. The figure in the second-story window may be Wilbur.

Mutually respecting, mutually challenging.

Quietly Making Ready

With no apparent intention, Wilbur and Orville acquired during the 1890s the skills that would be required to answer the question of flight.

Their printing work taught mechanism and precision. Their bicycle shop introduced them to strong, lightweight construction. That shop, profitably run, secured their financial independence – providing leisure time that could be turned to their own interests.

Equally, they had the proper habits of mind. From childhood, their parents had inculcated in them habits of intellectual curiosity and hard work. Wilbur had to an exceptional degree the engineer's capacity to keep the whole and the parts of a problem, and the relationship of parts to whole, clearly and consistently in mind. Orville had been a prize mathematics student; he was naturally inventive.

Both were physically fit – an often-overlooked point. Flying gliders takes considerable body control; dragging the glider back up the sand dunes at Kitty Hawk after each descent required strength and endurance.

They had – and this is central – the unqualified support of their extremely close family. Whatever Bishop Wright, their father, or Katharine, their sister, knew of aviation, they had and maintained full faith in Wilbur and Orville's work.

And they had each other. Wilbur and Orville meshed as collaborators – mutually respecting, mutually challenging – a juncture suggested by the name by which they are known to history: the Wright brothers.

▶ Opposite: Orville and Wilbur, about 1910.
▶ Above: Wilbur at work on a lathe in the Wright bicycle shop.

Where the work got done

The Wright Bicycle Shop was moved to Greenfield Village in Dearborn, Michigan, years after the brothers' success. Orville worked with Henry Ford to arrange the move.

Chanute began as mentor and sounding board for the Wrights.

Octave Chanute, Promoter

I n May 1900, Wilbur wrote a letter of introduction that began, "For some years I have been afflicted with the belief that flight is possible to man." Consider "afflicted." To this point in his life, Wilbur in his own mind had undertaken no very serious endeavor. To redirect his life, he was undertaking an endeavor that almost no one took seriously. He did this not because he had got hold of the idea of flight, but because the idea of flight had got hold of him.

Wilbur's letter was mailed to one of the few men in America who shared his affliction, a Paris-born civil engineer named Octave Chanute. Chanute had considerable professional standing – he designed the Chicago Stockyards and the first bridge to span the Missouri River, and had been president of the American Association for the Advancement of Science. In retirement, Chanute pursued aviation, building and testing gliders. Once, a pilotless Chanute glider sailed 359 feet down the Indiana Dunes.

Wilbur's first letter to Chanute initiated a regular correspondence. Chanute began as mentor and sounding board for the Wrights. He sponsored Wilbur's appearances before engineering audiences. He helped with the drudge work of mathematical computations.

Chanute ended as sadly non-comprehending. As the Wrights neared a solution, he no longer grasped what they were talking about. Indeed, by 1902, there may have been no other person who could have understood what the Wrights were doing. By then, they had taken their problem over the horizon with nothing to bring them safely home except a wing and prayer. Fortunately, they knew how to design wings. And their father was a bishop.

▶ Above: Octave Chanute.
▶ Opposite: Wilbur's May 13, 1900, letter to Chanute.

Manufacturers of Van Cleve
Bicycles St. Clair

Wright Cycle Company

1127 West Third Street.

DAYTON, OHIO. *May 13, 1900*

Mr. Octave Chanute, Esq.,

Chicago, Ill.

Dear Sir:

For some years I have been afflicted with
the belief that flight is possible to man. My disease has
increased in severity and I feel that it will soon cost
me an increased amount of money if not my life. I have
been trying to arrange my affairs in such a way that I can
devote my entire time for a few months to experiment in this
field.

My general ideas of the subject are similar those held by
most practical experimenters, to wit: that what is chiefly needed is
skill rather than machinery. The flight of the buzzard and similar
sailors is a convincing demonstration of the value of skill,
and the partial needlessness of motors. It is possible to fly with
out motors, but not without knowledge & skill. This I conceive to
be fortunate, for man, can by reason of his greater intellect, can
more reasonably hope to equal birds in knowledge, than to equal
nature in the perfection of her machinery.

Assuming then that Lillienthall was correct in his idea
of the principles on which man should proceed, I conceive that
his failure was due chiefly to the inadequacy of his method, and
of his apparatus. As to his method, the fact that in five
years time he spent only about five hours, altogether, in actual
flight is sufficient to show that his method was inadequate.
The simplest intellectual or acrobatic feats could never be ac-

Seeking shade

The Wright glider provided good protection from the hot North Carolina sun. In the photo are (L-R): Octave Chanute, Orville, Wilbur, aviation enthusiasts Augustus M. Herring, an unidentified man and George C. Spratt.

Hard at work

The Wright bicycle shop reflected the orderly approach the Wrights brought to all endeavors. Ed Sines (middle) was among the workers at the shop.

Airplane factory

The general machine shop of the
Wright factory in Dayton, 1911.

Woodworking

The Wright factory woodworking department, with Don Farrell, Frank Queen and Bill Conover.

3

The Problem

▶ Previous page: The Wright glider, fighting to become airborne at Kitty Hawk, 1901.
▶ Above: Harriet Silliman, Katharine Wright and Orville Wright on a drive in a St. Louis automobile, 1903.
▶ Opposite: After the aviation years, Orville vacationed on Lambert Island in Georgian Bay, Midland, Ontario. The dog's name is Scipio. They were joined by travel writer Vilhjalmur Stefansson, who is in the back of the canoe.

In a world of gradations, flight is the all-or-nothing proposition.

Compared to a Boat

The British aviation writer Charles Gibbs-Smith points out that most forms of transportation develop by increment. Someone sitting on the bank of a river sees a log float by; they imagine that floating on that log would be an easier way of getting downstream. Next, they realize that paddling with their hands improves speed and control. Then they hollow out the log. Then they substitute a paddle for the hand. Each step is an immediately usable improvement over what already exists. In this way, the log eventually becomes the Queen Elizabeth II.

Similarly, the horse leads to the rider leads to the horse-and-cart leads to the horseless carriage leads to a BMW. Each progression of improvements pushes the development of skills – the sailmaker's craft, the wheelwright's precision – thereby fostering further improvement.

Flight, Gibbs-Smith noted, offers no such "halfway" houses. Either the thing flies, or the thing does not fly. A hollowed log has some utility; a thing that does not fly has none. In a world of gradations, flight is the all-or-nothing proposition. That is why, at heart, flight did not come through a series of improvements, but from a leap of faith.

Flying high, eventually

Best known for flight, Dayton began as a city of rivers, which drew the first settlers from Cincinnati. The Main Street bridge, seen here from an airplane in 1910, spans the Great Miami River.

Shakespeare had it right. Thin air.

The Tempest

Our revels now are ended. These our actors,
As I foretold you, were all spirits and
Are melted into air, into thin air.

As *The Tempest* ends, its characters "are melted into air, into thin air." Elsewhere, Shakespeare refers to "the biting air" and "the mid-range air" and of those who, forlorn, try to sustain themselves on "the air of empty promise." One can have an air, get some air, come up for air or air it out. Air can be happy, hushed, intimate, native, serious, suspended or thine own. The writer Gerard Manley Hopkins wrote somewhere of "world-mothering air." But in terms of aviation, Shakespeare's first thought had it right. Thin air.

In 1901, Wilbur Wright spoke to the Western Society of Engineers in Chicago. He spoke of his and Orville's early glider experiments. He began by using a piece of paper to give those present a sense of how unruly a beast the air currents are:

> *If I take this piece of paper, and after placing it parallel to the ground, quickly let it fall, it will not settle steadily down as a staid, sensible piece of paper ought to do, but it insists on contravening every recognized rule of decorum, turning over and darting hither and thither in the most erratic manner, much after the style of an untrained horse. Yet this is the style of steed that men must learn to manage before flying can become an everyday sport.*

That is, they must learn to make a craft that will move and direct itself supported by nothing more than Shakespeare's thin air.

▶ Above and opposite: The wind-blown dunes of Kitty Hawk were distant, stark and lonely.

Catching the wind

The Wrights tested their gliders as kites before attempting to ride them.

He was daring, persistent and wrong.

The Birdman of Germany

O f their precursors in flight, the Wright brothers admired most the German, Otto Lilienthal. Lilienthal was an engineer, concerted in his efforts to fly. His *Birdflight as the Basis for Aviation*, published in 1889, reflected a decade spent studying the flight of birds.

Warming to his text, Lilienthal built a succession of gliders, testing them personally. Seeing Lilienthal outfitted, one reporter wrote, "So perfectly was the machine fitted together that it was impossible to find a single loose cord or brace, and the cloth everywhere was under such tension that the whole machine rang like a drum when rapped with the knuckles." It was, the reporter added, not a toy but a machine to fly with. In seven years, Lilienthal made 2,000 glides, launching himself down a hillside.

He was daring, persistent and wrong. He was wrong in approach: Airborne, Lilienthal strove to maintain his balance by rapid shifts of his legs and hips; no craft large enough to carry passengers could be so controlled. He was wrong in fact: Lilienthal painstakingly developed tables showing how lift varied with wing shape. His tables became standard – indeed, became a roadblock, as the tables were incorrect.

And he failed in outcome. On August 9, 1896, Lilienthal fell 50 feet to the ground, dying of his injuries. Orville, 26, was ill with typhoid fever when the news reached Dayton; Wilbur read the accounts. Later, Wilbur said Lilienthal's death prompted his own active interest in flying. In time, the Wrights would retrace Lilienthal's steps. They would invent a better means of control. They would devise more accurate tables of lift. They admired the German not for his success, but for his discipline and for his courage.

▶ Above: Otto Lilienthal.
▶ Opposite: Samuel Langley.

Aerodynamically, his craft resembled 'a handful of mortar.'

Smithsonian Gentleman

In pursuing flight, the Wrights risked loss of time and money, injury and even death. For a decade before the brothers' entry into the field, Samuel Pierpont Langley had risked something more. Langley was the long-time director of the Smithsonian Institution; as such, he was among the most reputable men in America. Langley risked his reputation by his insistence that man could fly.

Beginning in 1887, Langley designed and flew more than 100 model aircraft, achieving only such success as was minimally necessary to maintaining his optimism. Optimism was needed. Langley had done a poor job of thinking through the problem of flight. He tested model aircraft because he believed – wrongly – that a working model could be scaled up to a full-sized machine. It can't. If you double the length and depth of a wing, you increase its lifting surface by a factor of four. But an aircraft is a three-dimensional object; if you double the length, width and height of the whole machine, you increase its weight by a factor of eight. The smaller version might fly; the larger one won't. Why so elementary a fact never occurred to a scientist as good as Langley has never been explained.

In 1900, Langley secured $50,000 from the U.S. Army to build a full-sized flying machine, which he called the Aerodrome. On October 7, 1903, the Aerodrome slid down a launch ramp facing the Potomac River and landed nose-first in the water. On December 8, 1903, a repaired craft slid down the launch ramp and landed nose-first in the water. An observer noted that, aerodynamically, Langley's craft resembled "a handful of mortar."

Langley's second failure came just nine days before the Wrights' first flight; well publicized, it added much to the public's severe skepticism about aviation.

Making it work

The Wrights admired Lilienthal, but rejected his data in favor of their own, which they soon put into practical use in designing their 1902 glider – shown in this retouched photo.

Helping hands make light work

The 1902 Wright glider being launched cautiously on the dunes at Kitty Hawk. A stiff wind provided the lift; a man on each wing stabilized the glider.

Skimming the sand

In addition to steady wind, Kitty Hawk offered deep sand for soft landings. The 1902 glider in flight.

Progress

The Wrights' 1902 glider
proved that mastery of the
air was within their grasp.

Soaring

The graceful 1902
glider, with the
hangar and cabin of
the Kitty Hawk camp
in the background.

4

The Solution

Wilbur studied the gliding birds of Ohio.

Had I Wings Like a Dove

S hortly after Wilbur learned of Otto Lilienthal's gliding death, he took down from the family book-
shelf a volume called *Animal Mechanism* and considered the flight of birds. He shared his speculations
with his brother. Orville later wrote, "If the bird's wings would sustain it in the air without the use of any
muscular effort, we did not see why man could not be sustained by the same means."

Wilbur wrote the Smithsonian Institution for a list of books on flight; he and Orville read up on the
subject, assessing what others had tried and how they had failed. Lilienthal failed, Wilbur concluded,
because he lacked an effective means of maintaining balance. His wings had tipped up, increasing the
resistance of the wind, robbing him of forward movement and causing his fall.

Looking for ideas, Wilbur studied hawks and buzzards, the gliding birds of Ohio. He realized that
birds in glide correct their lateral balance by twisting their wingtips. If a bird wants to lower its right
wing, it flexes the right wingtip down; air currents then strike the upper side of the wing, pushing it back
to level.

Wilbur had the insight; Orville had the solution. He devised a mechanism that allowed the wingtips
of a glider to be flexed on command. The Wrights called it "wing warping." They tested the idea
successfully on a five-foot glider. What they needed next was a glider large enough to carry a pilot and a
place where the winds blew free.

▶ Previous page: The balance mechanism holds upright one of many wing shapes the Wrights
tested in miniature.

▶ Opposite: Wilbur's study of birds in flight led to mechanical wing warping.
▶ Above: The 1902 glider, with the Kitty Hawk camp in the distance.

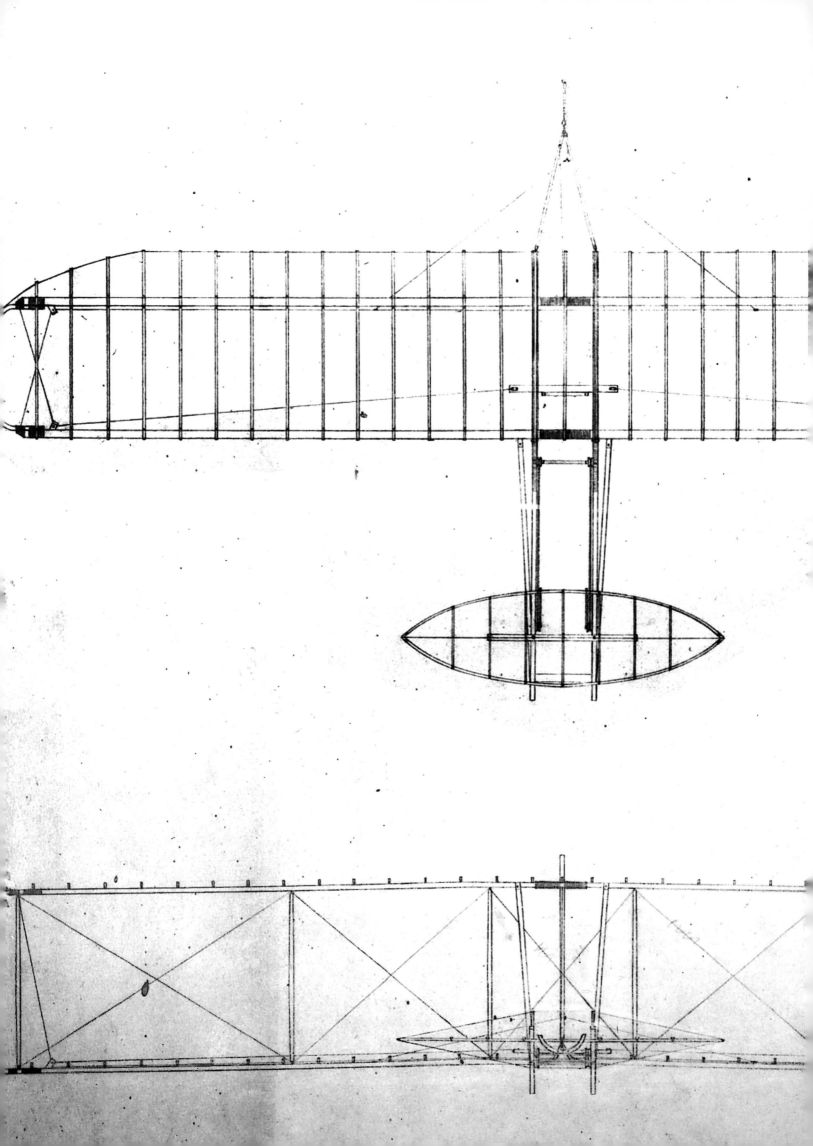

Putting it on paper

The brothers were careful to document
their work. These diagrams show one
of the Wright gliders on paper.

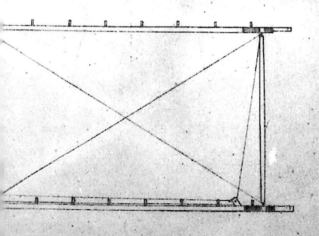

Half vacation, half scientific outing.

Nowhere to Go But Up

Waves, sand and time created the barrier islands that run north to south along the ocean coast of North Carolina. Near the northern end of one island is a settlement, Kitty Hawk, that Wilbur and Orville would make famous.

The Wrights hit upon it in 1900 while looking for a site to conduct their gliding experiments. Wilbur sought details from William J. Tate, a minor public official in Kitty Hawk. Tate replied optimistically, "You could, for instance, get a stretch of sandy land one mile by five with a bare hill in the center 80 feet high, not a tree or bush anywhere to break the evenness of the wind current."

Steady winds to fill the fabric of their wings; unruffled sands for soft landing. The spot was isolated – in decent weather, reachable only by boat; in rough weather, unreachable. The weather, except for the occasional hurricane, was fair. Tate informed Wilbur that as there were no living quarters on the island, the brothers would have to pitch a tent.

The Wrights' first trip to Kitty Hawk was half vacation, half scientific outing. Writing to his father before departing, Wilbur noted that flight was "almost the only great problem that has not been pursued by a multitude of investigators." As such, it might prove possible for the Wrights to advance the field. In consequence, Wilbur said, "I think there is a slight possibility of achieving fame and fortune from it."

▶ Opposite: (L-R) Octave Chanute, amateur aviator Edward Huffaker, Orville and Wilbur share a rare moment of leisure at the Kitty Hawk camp.

▶ Above: Orville shows off the stubby, short-winged 1901 glider.

Distant and desolate

The view from the 1900 camp was mostly sand dunes, with the Kitty Hawk settlement in the background. The sparsely populated area was difficult to reach.

The bad news was that their glider simply didn't glide.

The Taste of Failure

Everybody said flight was a fool idea. At moments during 1900 and 1901, Wilbur and Orville might have agreed. Those years marked the Wrights' first two summer visits to Kitty Hawk, where they faced a shortage of food, a surplus of mosquitoes and disappointment in their results.

Wilbur arrived first, on September 10, 1900. He'd hustled most of their unassembled glider from Dayton to Elizabeth City, North Carolina, where he purchased the longer boards need for the spars. He then journeyed on to Kitty Hawk, where he informed the locals – many of them named Tate – that he intended to fly his glider just as soon as his brother arrived.

Orville soon did. The good news of their two-week stay was that their system of wing warping proved dependable on a full-sized glider. The bad news was that their glider simply didn't glide. Indeed, it produced less than half of the lift they had expected.

Back in Dayton, they puzzled over this. The figures for lift had been drawn from Lilienthal's tables. The Wrights had put their faith in these figures, so they tinkered with their craft and took an "improved" model back to Kitty Hawk in 1901.

The new model did worse.

As they left North Carolina that year, Wilbur said, "We considered our experiments a failure. At this time I made the prediction that people would sometime fly, but that it would not be within our lifetime." Orville went Wilbur one better. If Lilienthal's tables were correct, he said, "Not within a thousand years would man ever fly."

► Opposite: As a favor to Chanute, the Wrights helped Edward Huffaker test his glider, the "$1,000 Beauty," at Kitty Hawk in 1901. The wreckage of the glider is shown here.
► Above: The Wrights sustained their interest in both gliders and Kitty Hawk. Orville returned to test this model in 1911.

Still grounded

An 'improved' 1901 glider – seen here from inside the
Kitty Hawk hangar – was based on the Lilienthal data.
Its poor performance discouraged the Wrights.

(1) Designation of Surface.		#1	#2	#3	#4	#5	#6	#7	#8	#9	#10	#11	#12	#13	#15	#16	#17
Area in sq. in.		6	6	6	6	6	6	6	6	6	6	6	6	6	6	6	6
Lift begins		0	0	0	-5½	-4¼	-3½	-3	-2¾	-2¾	-3	-2¾	-2½	-4	-4¼	-4	-3¾
Angle of incidence	0°	0	0	0	7½	6	5¾	8⅛	8	8	7⅞	7	6¼	8¼	4½	4¼	4
" "	2½°	2¼	5½	7¼	11¼	8¾	8½	17⅞	17½	15¾	18¼	16¼	13½	15	8	6⅞	6¾
" "	5°	4⅞	11½	13¾	15	12¾	11¾	25	23½	22½	26½	25	22¾	22¼	12½	10⅛	9¼
" "	7½°	8	17¼	20½	18¾	16	15½	31½	29½	27¾	33½	32	32	27¾	16	14¼	13½
" "	10°	11½	22¼	27	22¾	19⅞	19	38½	39	39	36	37	39	29¼	19⅞	19	17¼
" "	12½°	15	27½	30½	27	24	22¾	52	49¾	46½	36½	37	44	30½	24	22⅛	21¾
" "	15°	19	31¼	32	32½	28¼	27¼	61	55½	50½	38	38¾	46½	32½	29¼	28	26
" "	17½°	23¼	32	33	37½	33	32¼	63½	56¼	51	39	41⅞	45½	34¼	36¾	33	31
" "	20°	27	33¾	33¼	42	39	36¼	60½	52	48¾	41	42	44	35½	40½	37⅛	35¾
" "	25°	34½	33¼	32¾	49½	47	44½	50¼	47½	44	44½	41½	41½	36	49	47¾	44½
" "	30°	38¼	31¾	32½	57½	54¾	49½	46¾	44	41½	41	39¼	39¼	37½	56	52	49½
" "	35°	37¼	30	32½	58½	55¼	60	45	42¼	40¾	39¾	38¾	38½	—	52½	48	45½
" "	40°	29½	28	32½	47½	40	38½	43½	41	40	39	38¼	38	—	38	34	32¾
" "	45°	27	27	32½	35	33¾	30¾	41¾	39¼	38¼	38¼	37	36½	30½	30½	29¾	29
Data [illegible]		[illegible] Lifts or Rectangular Pressure. [illegible]															

The area of the normal plane against which they were balanced was 8 sq. in., or ⅓ more than of the surfaces whose lifts were being measured.

► Above: Back to the drawing board. Having decided that the existing data on lift was incorrect, the Wrights began compiling their own.

► Opposite: The Wrights' handmade wind tunnel was the key piece of equipment in early studies of aerodynamics.

The Wrights decided the 'book' was wrong.

Self-Reliance

───⟫·◇·⟪───

S ome school math books give the answers in the back. The student works a problem, then checks the back of the book. If the student's answer differs from the back-of-the-book answer, the student assumes his or her answer to be wrong. Their first two summers at Kitty Hawk, the Wrights got answers that differed from the back of the book. Their gliders' sluggish behavior in the field at Kitty Hawk was at odds with the results Lilienthal's tables predicted.

The Wrights did an unusual thing. They decided the "book" was wrong. It was an act of intellectual courage, the point at which the Wrights finally launched themselves not from earth, but from everything known or supposed before. Wilbur later wrote, "Having set out with absolute faith in the existing scientific data, we were driven to doubt one thing after another, till finally, after two years of experiment, we cast it all aside, and decided to rely on our own investigations."

They set out to create their own tables. To do so, they built in their bike shop the first wind tunnel specially designed for aeronautical research. They tested in it dozens of wing shapes, compiling data on how performance differed with length, width and curvature. They worked through the fall of 1901, an emotional high point that prompted Orville to write, "Wilbur and I could hardly wait for the morning to come to get at something that interested us. *That's* happiness."

By January 1902, the Wrights had gathered, they estimated, 100 times more information on wing design than anyone previous. With this data, they designed a new glider for the 1902 season. Where their earlier gliders had been stubby, clumsy-looking things, this new glider had wings that were long, slender and tapering. The new glider looked like an airplane.

Working from known technology

Before building a wind tunnel, the Wrights furthered their understanding of aerodynamics by mounting model wings on a bicycle and riding into the wind. This test-equipment reproduction is on display at Carillon Historical Park in Dayton.

The glider flights confirmed the wind-tunnel data.

Triumph!

At Kitty Hawk in 1902, all things thrived. At their camp, the batten boards Orville and Wilbur had nailed to their shed kept out rain and drifting sand. Indoors, they had beds instead of cots to sleep on; better water from a new well. They adapted a bike to running over the sand, cutting their round trip to Kitty Hawk from three hours to one. For once, the island was mosquito-free.

And their new glider soared. It skimmed over the dunes as though those sandy hills were its natural home. In two months the Wrights made more than one thousand glides; the longest came October 23, when Wilbur went 622.5 feet in 26 seconds, the longest flight ever achieved. Dan Tate shared the enthusiasm, saying of the Wrights' 1902 machine, "All she needs is a coat of feathers to make her light, and she will stay in the air indefinitely."

The glider flights confirmed the accuracy of the wind-tunnel data. Only then did Wilbur and Orville consider the next step. Years later, Orville wrote, "When we were carrying on our wind-tunnel work we had no thought of ever trying to build a powered aeroplane.... But after we had demonstrated in a glider that our tables were correct, we saw it would not be hard to design a man-carrying powered aeroplane."

Before breaking camp in 1902, the Wrights sketched out the requirements of a flying machine. They would, they calculated, need 520 square feet of wing surface, an engine of eight or more horsepower and a weight limit of 625 pounds. Including Wilbur or Orville, who weighed pretty much the same.

▶ Opposite: The 1902 glider.
▶ Above: A 1902 display of wing-warping to guide the glider was captured on film.

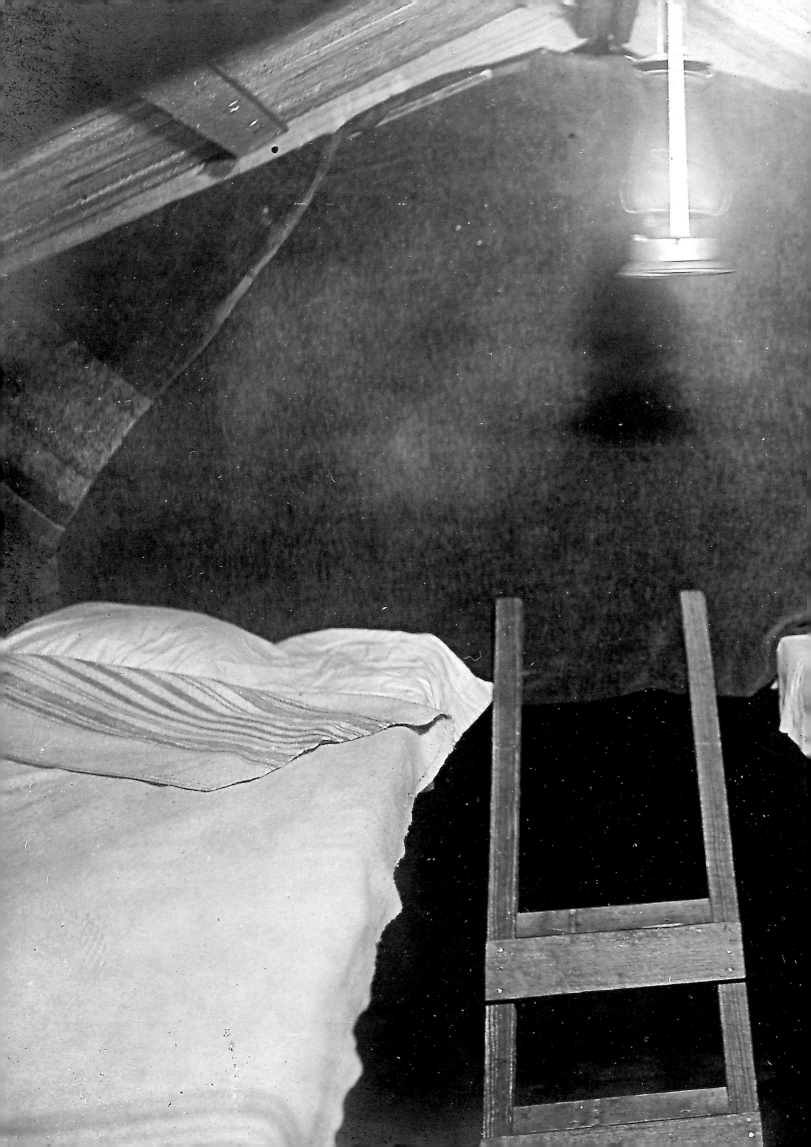

Cramped but cozy

A bedroom loft at Kitty Hawk was an improvement over the cots they had used during previous stays.

A Propeller is a Spinning Wing

The real work of flight was not the piece-by-piece shaping in the bike shop of each airplane part. The real work was solving flight as an intellectual puzzle – puzzles through which Wilbur and Orville argued in the parlor of their home at 7 Hawthorn Street. A niece, Ivonette, recalled, "One of them would make a statement. There'd be a long pause, and then the other one would make a statement, and then the other one would say, 'Tisn't, tisn't either,' and then it would be 'Tis too,' 'Tisn't either,' and then there'd be a long pause again."

The questions they addressed were, in a Mark Twain phrase, "interesting, but tough." In early 1903, they tackled design of the propeller. In a charmingly naive move, they presented themselves at the old Dayton Public Library on Third Street and asked for books on ship's propellers. No such books were available. Propellers for ships were designed not from theory but empirically; that is, from accumulated trial and error.

Orville and Wilbur had no alternative but to think the problem through for themselves. Wilbur later wrote: "Nothing about a propeller, or the medium in which it acts, stand still for a moment. The thrust depends upon the speed and the angle at which the blade strikes the air; the angle at which the blade strikes the air depends upon the speed at which the propeller is turning, the speed at which the machine is traveling forward, and the speed at which the air is slipping backward; (while) the slip of the air backward depends upon the thrust exerted by the propeller, and the amount of air acted upon. When any of these changes, it changes all the rest."

On and on, they argued. They filled five notebooks with sketches and computations. The problem became "simple" – Wilbur's term – when they realized that a propeller was really just a spinning wing. As such, it would behave in accordance with the information on wing design gathered with their wind tunnel. From this data, Wilbur and Orville designed the first aircraft propellers. To build each, they laminated three pieces of wood together, then worked them into shape with hand tools. Aviation historian Peter Jakab noted, "Before the Wright propeller there was none like it, and after it there were none that were different."

▶ Opposite: An early propeller.
▶ Above: Student pilot S.M. Crane examines a propeller at the Montgomery, Alabama, aviation
school established by the Wrights in 1910. The site later became Maxwell Air Force Base.

Detailed handiwork

Refined propellers were produced by the Wright Company, with finishes carefully applied by hand.

'I knew exactly how to do it. I did it.'

Charlie Taylor, Mechanic

C harlie Taylor had a sad life redeemed by the fact that it was he who built the engine that flew at Kitty Hawk in 1903.

Taylor was a mechanic on Dayton's west side. The Wrights jobbed work to him from their bicycle shop – he machined some coaster brakes they had designed – and on June 15, 1901, they hired him full-time at $16.50 a week.

The general story is that the Wrights built their own engine because they could not find a commercial one with a sufficient power-to-weight ratio. At least as likely is the possibility that the Wrights, being stingy, didn't want to spend the money and had Taylor to help them.

Taylor had previously built just one engine. Later, he gave a succinct summary of his efforts: "I knew exactly how to do it. I did it." He did it despite the fact that the Wrights had only two pieces of machining equipment, a drill press and a lathe. This posed problems. To create the camshaft, for example, Taylor used the drill press to drill out an outline of the shaft on a piece of steel. This he chiseled free, then turned on the lathe until a camshaft emerged.

The finished engine was a crude thing. It had no spark plugs: A low-tension magneto sent a current down a copper strip that touched the cylinders. It had no cooling system: After five minutes, the engine's valves glowed red hot. And it had only two speeds, one of which was "off." On December 17, 1903, Taylor's engine launched Orville into the skies. Four weeks later, Orville and Wilbur gave him a $1.50-a-week raise.

▶ Opposite: Charlie Taylor in the Wright bike shop on West Third Street in Dayton.
▶ Above: In later years.

One of a kind

Taylor built the engine for the 1903 Wright
Flyer using only a lathe and a drill press
for machining tools. The engine had two
speeds, one of which was 'off.'

Milton Wright would have none of it. Nor would his sons.

Delay

In 1903, Bishop Milton Wright was embroiled in controversy within the United Brethren Church. He believed that the overseer of the church's publishing operation was skimming funds. Others in the church hoped to paper the matter over; Milton Wright would have none of it. Nor would his sons. Wilbur and Orville were not churchgoers, but they rushed to help: Wilbur conducted an independent audit of the books and published a defense of his father's position.

This delayed their departure for Kitty Hawk. By the time they reached the seashore, the ocean had turned gray and leaden. They flew their craft first as a glider – it performed beautifully – then added the engine and propellers and continued testing. On November 5, a propeller shaft cracked; it was sent back to Dayton for repair. The Wrights waited; it turned colder. They awoke November 19 and the ponds near their camp had frozen over. Wilbur wrote home:

> *We are entirely comfortable, and have no trouble keeping warm at nights. In addition to the classification of last year, to wit, 1, 2, 3 and 4 blanket nights, we now have 5 blanket nights, & 5 blankets & 2 quilts. Next comes 5 blankets, 2 quilts & fire; then 5, 2, fire and hot-water jug. This is as far as we have gone so far.... We intend to be comfortable while we are here.*

The repaired shaft arrived and soon cracked again. This time, Orville escorted it back to Dayton personally. Wilbur remained at camp, studying German grammar. Orville returned. By the second week in December, all was ready.

▶ Opposite: There were few idle moments at the Kitty Hawk camp. Wilbur, shown here, and Orville usually found plenty to do.
▶ Above: Wilbur scours dishes in the sand.

Impeccably organized

The Wrights' Kitty Hawk kitchen was clean and well organized. Canned goods – with plenty of peaches – were filed on shelves, as were eggs, which Orville numbered according to sequence laid.

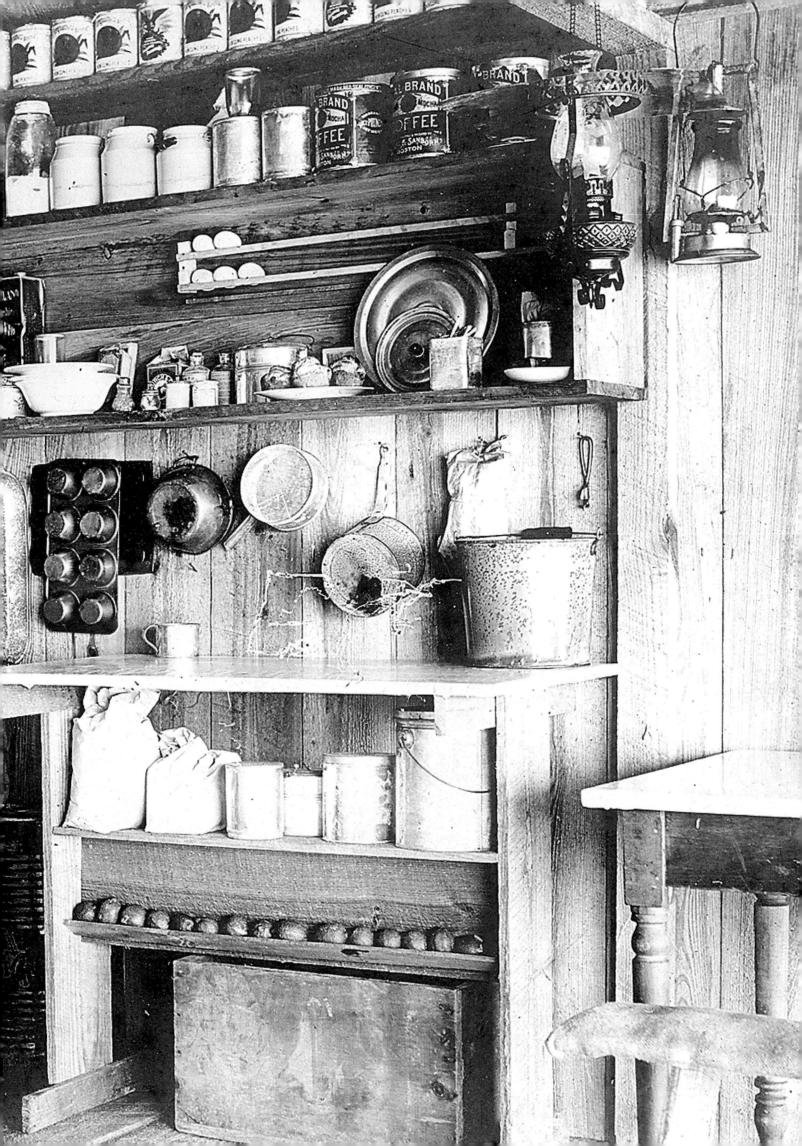

They held on to each other's hands.

December 17, 1903

On December 17, the wind was up. At camp, the Wrights hung out the flag they used to signal their intention to fly. William Tate, the Wrights' semi-host during their visits to Kitty Hawk, had decided the wind was too strong, so he did not check to see if the flag was out. He missed the show.

On hand were members of the federal lifesaving station at nearby Kill Devil Hills, who helped the Wrights slide their aircraft over the sands. One lifesaver said of the brothers just prior to launch, "We couldn't help notice how they held on to each other's hand, sorta like two folks parting who weren't sure they'd ever see one another again."

The craft was launched by sliding down a 50-foot rail of two-by-fours. Wilbur set up their camera pointed toward the end of the rail. He instructed one of the lifesavers, John T. Daniels, to trigger the camera just as the aircraft reached the rail's end. Daniels had never seen an airplane. Quite probably, he had never used a camera. He did as instructed and took what is likely the most famous amateur photograph of all time – of Orville leaving the ground on the first-ever heavier-than-air flight.

Orville flew just 120 feet. Of the three remaining flights that day, Wilbur's of 852 feet was the longest. After that flight, a gust flipped the aircraft over. Damaged, it never flew again.

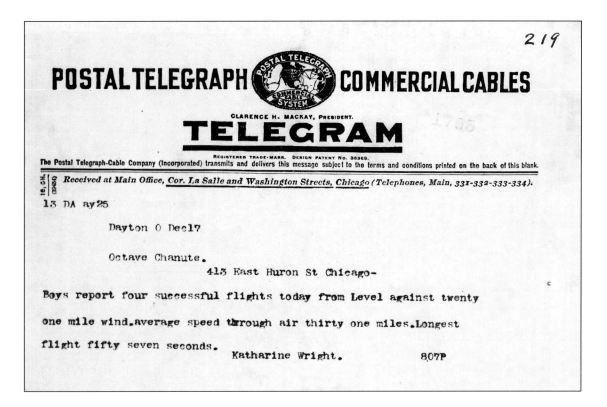

POSTAL TELEGRAPH COMMERCIAL CABLES

CLARENCE H. MACKAY, PRESIDENT.

TELEGRAM

REGISTERED TRADE-MARK. DESIGN PATENT No. 36369.

The Postal Telegraph-Cable Company (Incorporated) transmits and delivers this message subject to the terms and conditions printed on the back of this blank.

Received at Main Office, Cor. La Salle and Washington Streets, Chicago (Telephones, Main, 331-332-333-334).

13 DA ay 25

    Dayton O Dec17

    Octave Chanute.

        413 East Huron St Chicago-

Boys report four successful flights today from Level against twenty

one mile wind.average speed through air thirty one miles.Longest

flight fifty seven seconds.
        Katharine Wright.   807P

▶ Opposite: The dunes of Kitty Hawk.
▶ Above: Katharine wired Octave Chanute, telling him of her brothers' success.

First flight

The Wrights' first successful powered flight, on December 17, 1903, covered a distance of 120 feet. Orville was the pilot. Three more flights were made that day. Wilbur's, of 852 feet, was the longest. After that flight, a gust of wind flipped the aircraft over, damaging it. It never flew again.

Tough guys

The federal life-saving crew at nearby Kill Devil Hills was photographed by the Wrights during their 1900 stay. The crew's Captain Payne is pictured here third from the right. In 1903, crew members were the first to witness powered flight.

The camp

The hangar and cabin at Kitty Hawk were built with utility in mind. Braces steadied the buildings against the wind and shifting dunes.

Everything in its place

Orville (front) and Wilbur spent a lot of time in their Kitty Hawk hangar, repairing or modifying their work. This 1903 photo shows that the front and rear walls were hinged for access and ventilation.

An ill wind

Damaged after its fourth flight, the 1903 Wright Flyer had a one-day career. It now hangs in the National Air and Space Museum in Washington, D.C.

5

Closer to Home

'Dayton Boys Emulate the Great Santos-Dumont.'

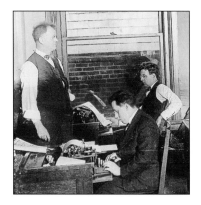

An Editor Misses the Point

With flight achieved, Wilbur and Orville telegraphed word of their success to Dayton. The Wright family conveyed the boys' triumph to the local press.

One Dayton newspaper ran the page-one headline: "Dayton Boys Emulate the Great Santos-Dumont." The great Santos-Dumont, first name Alberto, was a Brazilian who pursued aviation and notoriety in France. In 1900 he rigged an engine to a hot-air balloon and in no very modest way putt-putted it around the Eiffel Tower, to the delight and bedazzlement of the noonday crowds below.

The headline suggests how little clue the world had to the Wrights' achievement: an editor in Dayton could not conceive of the difference between Santos-Dumont taking a blimp for a joyride and the Wrights opening the age of flight. The editor's misunderstanding proved common: Not for five years would the world at large believe the Wright brothers had flown.

▶ Previous page: Flying over Huffman Prairie, also known as Simms Station, near Dayton.
▶ Above: The *Dayton Daily News* city room, about 1900.
▶ Opposite: Two days after the fact, the *Dayton Daily News* ran Katharine's telegram, but still failed to understand its implications: The story appeared on page 12.
▶ Following pages: By 1908, the world's press understood what the Wrights had accomplished, and the story was front-page news.

WRIGHT FLYER.

Clever Device of Bishop Wright's Sons.

REMARKABLE ACCOMPLISHMENT OF TWO OF DAYTON'S INDUSTRIOUS YOUNG MEN.

Gratifying Success Reported With Excellent Prospects of Achieving Complete Success With Their New Flying Machine.

Bishop Milton Wright of this city has received a telegram from his sons, Wilbur and Orville Wright, who are at Kitty Hawks, North Carolina, the fourth autumn, experimenting in gliding through the air on aeroplane of their own make, and regulated by devices of their own invention. The telegram says that they have had gratifying success with their flying machine, built the present year by them in this city. The Wright Flyer, as they call it, is a double-decked, curved aeroplane, driven by a small but powerful gasoline motor with aerial screw propellers. The telegram is as follows:

Kitty Hawk, N. C., Dec. 17.

Bishop M. Wright, 7 Hawthorn street.—We have made four successful flights this morning from level

here to visit Miss Myrtle Brandon the first of this week.

Pleasant Hill Grange held an election and installation of officers at the hall on Main street last Saturday. The election was in the forenoon, after which an oyster dinner was served in the hall, and in the afternoon the officers were installed by Col. W. M. Williamson, of Piqua, O.

Ralph Douthitt left for his home on Tuesday last in Pike county, after a stay of six or seven weeks with his brother, Walter, of this village.

Regular services will be held in the Christian church next Sunday morning and evening by the pastor, Rev. C. I. Dego. Topic of morning discourse, "The Babe of Bethlehem;" in the evening "The Passing of 1903."

Rev. Watson of Dayton held services in the Brethren church here last Sunday morning and evening. He will return next Sunday and commence his protracted meetings.

Mrs. Catherine Hartley of Little York, accompanied by her daughter-in-law, Mrs. Hettie Hartley, of Fidelity, visited relatives here the early part of this week.

W. L. Murton, who had been editing the Pleasant Hill Journal, left last week for Iowa, where he has secured employment in a newspaper office.

John Class of Little York was here the early part of this week visiting friends.

Nathan Hill and Mrs. Catherine Reiber attended the funeral of Charlotte Williams at Covington on last Tuesday.   UNCLE JAKE.

MEMORIAL SERVICES.

Grand Army Annual Gathering and Mournful Ceremonies.

The annual memorial services were held in G. A. R. hall at Hamilton last evening. Rev. E. M. McFadden, D. D., delivered the address, and the First Reformed quartet furnished the music in this very fine program:

Opening Hymn, "Nearer My God to Thee"—Quartet and Congregation.

Prayer—Chaplain.

Tribute of Respect to Deceased Comrades—Adjutant.

Duet. "Oh, Morning Land"

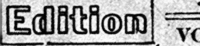
Last Edition

THE DAYTON

VOL. XXII. NO. 304.   DAYTON. OHIO. MOND

Daytonians Heralded As Conquerors of Air

Nine In Co

ECKERNFOR
—Nine persons
injured this mo
tween a passen
empty cars on
between Flens
dead and inju
towns along th

French Monoplanist Declares Wright Machine Superior to Anything Yet Invented.

WORLD WILL MARVEL AT AVIATION PROGRESS.

Daring of the American Aeronauts Stirs the French Press to Unstinted Praise.

SUCCESS APPLAUDED

(Bulletin.)

LE MANS, Aug. 10.—After two false starts, Wilbur Wright, the Dayton, O., aeroplainist, made a successful ascension here shortly before 8 o'clock this evening. The machine flew about two kilometres (1.24 miles) in one minute and 45 seconds, official time. Owing to the lateness of the hour Mr. Wright decided not to try a longer run. The flight was viewed by several thousand people.

LEMANS, France, Aug. 10.—Wilbur Wright of Dayton, O., who made a successful flight with his aeroplane last Saturday, divided this morning and this afternoon hovering over and testing his aeroplane and trying to ward off the active army of photographers who were clamoring to take a picture of himself and his aeroplane, the rights for which have already been contracted for.

A French army captain snapped his camera at the machine, but Mr. Wright insisted that the plates be handed over to him, or destroyed.

Mr. Wright may possibly attempt another flight this evening.

Wilbur Wright did not fly yesterday in his aeroplane, but remained in the his areoplane, but remained in the shed in which the machine is kept. A number of persons in automobiles and the inhabitants of Le Mans made pilrimages to Hunaudieres in the hope of obtaining a glimpse of the famous aeroplane aviator, but were disapointed, as Mr. Wright did not show himself, receiving only a few friends during the day.

The French press unites in spon-

HARVEST OF MONSTER

Six Automobilists Meet Death in Horrible Form While Seeking Pleasure.

BIG CAR PLUNGES DOWN EMBANKMENT

Near Toledo, Another Collides With Bridge, Third Is Struck by Train and Fourth Explodes.

DEATH'S TOLL LARGE,

While the Injured Number Eight and Two May Not Survive. San Francisco Woman and Logansport Business Man Killed. Priest and Importer Crushed to Death.

PAINESVILLE, O., Aug. 10.—Mrs. Mary Rowden, 65 years of age, and Mrs. Rose Beckwith, 43 years of age, were instantly killed and Fred Beckwith, 45 years old, was perhaps fatally injured, and Bessie Beckwith, 16 years of age, his daughter, badly bruised and burned by the explosion of a steam automobile at the foot of Stickey hill, about eight miles from Painesville, today.

Beckwith, accompanied by his mother-in-law, wife and daughter, was on his way home from their home at Windsor, O., to this city, and was running his machine at a rate of about eight miles an hour, when it exploded.

The occupants of the car were hurled in all directions. Mrs. Rowden, who was on the front seat with

One of the

Wilbur Wright.

DAILY NEWS.

AUGUST 10, 1908.   **PRICE ONE CENT.**

Washington, Aug. 10.—For Ohio: Showers tonight; Tuesday generally fair.

lain ision

rmany, Aug. 10. lled and many s a collision be- n and a train of ch line running nd Kiel. The re residents of

Tenement Occupants Hurt In Mad Panic

sed the World
ype of Aerial Craft

ht Brothers in Flight in a Gliding Machine.

ACRES OF BIG TENTS

Compose Camp Perry, Now the Busiest Spot in State of Ohio.

RIFLEMEN AFTER GLITTERING GOLD.

$50,000 Club House Furnishes All the Social Life and Refreshments Needed.

ARMY ON LAKE SHORE.

Mimic Warfare Begins at Fort Riley, Kan.—4600 Enlisted Men and 225 Officers Participate in the Military Maneuvers.

CAMP PERRY, O., Aug. 10.—What military officials declare will be the greatest military shooting tournament in the history of the world, was inaugurated on the Ohio rifle range at Camp Perry on the southern shore of Lake Erie, near Port Clinton, today.

Hundreds of contestants are on the ground from every state in the Union, Hawaii and the Philippines.

The Ohio matches, which will consume today, Tuesday, Wednesday and Thursday, were taken up this morning with teams organized from Troop A, Cleveland, and Troop B, Columbus, and from the Second, Third, Seventh and Eighth Regiments, Ohio aNtional Guard, on firing life.

The weather conditions are ideal and record-breaking scores are being made.

All the Ohio regimental rifle teams are encamped here for annual competition and Ohio State Rifle association matches, which opened today. The regimental team match was held first. The Second's team, commanded by

Scores are Carried Down Ladder from Blazing Buildings by Gotham Firemen.

MANY JUMP FROM UPPER WINDOWS

Crazed With Fear They Blindl Leap to Certain Death or Injury.

CHILDREN CREMATED

All Four the Members of On Family—Odor of Kerosen Leads to Belief of Incendiarism Thirteen Perished in Simila Fire in Same Locality Recently Pittsburg Blaze.

NEW YORK, Aug. 10.—Four children of one family dead and ten other persons seriously burned or injured the record of a fierce blaze that earl today swept through a crowded tene ment in East One Hundred an Twelfth street. Scores were carrie down ladders from the blazing build ing by firemen and wild scenes panic ensued as the scantily-clad ten ants rushed to the street. The dea were the children of Vinceno Saust janitor of the house, aged from months to 10 years. Frank Sausto dying from burns and Vinceno Saus and his wife are both suffering fro severe burns about the face and bod

As he leaped from a second sto window to escape the flames, Salv tore Logeforni had his right hip di focated, and several others were mo or less seriously injured either b burns or from contusions or lacer tions caused by leaping from window By the time the fire was discovere the flames had spread through t hallway and seized upon the stai cutting off escape. There were 8 persons in the building. When t firemen arrived ladders were run the sides of the building and 30 pe sons were rescued. Many would n wait for the ladders and crazed wi fear, leaped to the street below, re ceiving injuries more or less seve After hard work the firemen fire

The brothers, some said, were fools.

Huffman Prairie, 1904

The Wrights, one contemporary noted, flew at Kitty Hawk "just to prove their calculations." A nice phrase. The Wrights' gliders and early aircraft were, primarily, test instruments, flown so that the flaws of each might be identified and further data gathered. The four short flights in North Carolina showed their math was close enough: Heavier-than-air flight was possible. Barely. Wilbur's 852-foot flight at Kitty Hawk left the aircraft a long way shy of everyday practicality.

That practicality was achieved in 1904 and 1905 in a little-known place of great consequence, Huffman Prairie – an 85-acre cow pasture 10 miles east of Dayton. The Wrights moved their work to Huffman, likely, because it was near home and handy to the bike shop that supplied their parts and housed their repairs. The prairie was nearby, just a short ride on the interurban rail cars from Dayton to tiny Simms Station, and it was free. The field's owner, Torrence Huffman, president of the Fourth National Bank, allowed the Wrights to use the field on condition that they move his horses and cows out of the way before attempting to fly.

Flight was something Huffman did not anticipate. The brothers, he told a neighboring landowner, were "fools."

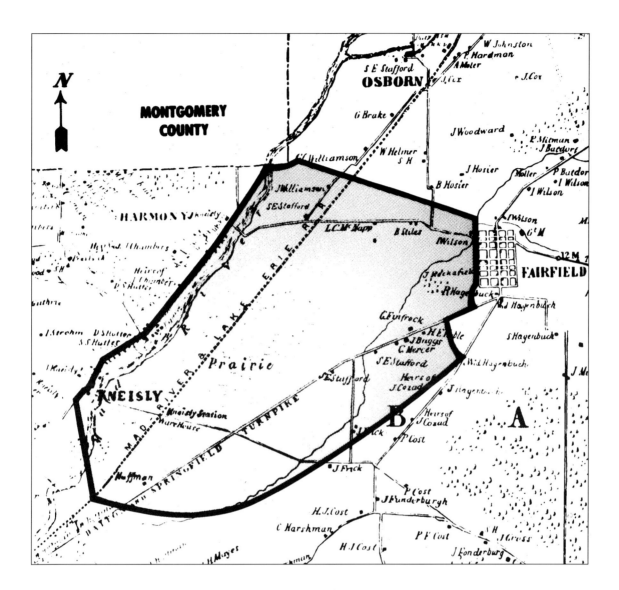

▶ Opposite: One of the first photos taken from an airplane shows the Wright hangar at Huffman Prairie. Despite its gentle name, the site was rough ground — full of ruts, hummocks and groundhog holes.

▶ Above: This period map of Huffman Prairie shows the villages of Fairfield and Osborn, which later combined to become Fairborn. Today, the prairie is part of Wright-Patterson Air Force Base, one of the world's largest military airfields.

Plenty to discuss
Orville (left) and Wilbur confer at
Huffman Prairie, 1904. The Flyer slid
on a track into its hangar.

Two minutes in the air and 11 days making repairs.

The Season of Their Discontent

For the Wrights, 1904 was uphill. In May, they decided to present their invention to the press. A small if doubting throng gathered. By close of day, all doubts had been confirmed. Twice, the aircraft failed at launch. The Wrights' machine, one reporter wrote, "was to have made a circle of the field, and, like a bird, alight with the wind." Unfortunately, he added, "The failure of the machine to go more than 25 feet prevented this."

There were problems more serious than the press. The winds near Dayton were not nearly as strong as at Kitty Hawk; day after day, the Wrights sat in their cow pasture waiting for a breeze sufficient for launching.

Launch brought more troubles. On October 15, a rough landing broke both propellers and the landing skids. Repairs took eight days. Thirty seconds into their next flight, the aircraft darted into the ground and broke a skid and a propeller. On November 1 after further repairs, the aircraft pulled its anchoring stake from the ground and began launching itself, with Orville clinging to its side. He wrenched his shoulder keeping the craft on the ground. The following day, four of five flights miscarried. The one successful launch led to a flight of 84 seconds; the final attempt ended with a broken tail. In these 18 days the Wrights managed two minutes in the air and 11 days making repairs.

▶ Opposite: Huffman Prairie offered the Wrights a place to perfect their aircraft — and their flying skills.
▶ Above: The Wrights' Huffman Prairie facilities had improved by 1910 with a larger, more open hangar, but the cows remained.

Where they got it right

At Huffman Prairie in 1904, the Wrights made more than 30 flights before surpassing Wilbur's best 1903 flight of 852 feet. The tower at the right was used with a weight-and-pulley system to help launches.

'The Germans doubt your achievements, as do the French.'

Skepticism

When Neal Armstrong took his small step onto the moon, millions watched his televised image. When Charles Lindbergh completed the first solo trans-Atlantic flight, tens of thousands greeted him in Paris. When Wilbur and Orville at Kitty Hawk made the first powered departure from the earth, their feat was witnessed by only a few souls.

Beyond that small assembly of Outer Banks lifeguards, perhaps the only people who believed heavier-than-air flight had been achieved were Milton and Katharine Wright, Charlie Taylor and the members of the Annual Club of the Ten Dayton Boys.

Nor did belief rush in. Fifteen months later, the March 1905 issue of *The Criterion* asked a series of experts the question: "Will man fly?" Most thought flight possible, though not yet. The Serbian-born electrical genius Nikola Tesla stated, "What we must have – and what we shall have some day – is a motor which will weigh the one-hundredth part of the motor we now use."

Skepticism was universal. On May 23, Chanute wrote the Wrights: "The Germans doubt your achievements, as do the French." As did, officially, the Americans. Three times in 1905, Wilbur wrote to the U.S. War Department, offering his government a world monopoly on flight for $25,000. Three times the War Department wrote back, telling Wilbur that he could not sell flight to the government as flight did not exist.

Lindbergh was the first to make the ocean crossing, but not the first to try. Each year, as aircraft and pilots improved, the expectation that one would eventually succeed grew. Likewise, Armstrong's step onto the moon followed a decade of bold forays into space. The Wrights, however, came with no history of previous, partial success. They came, in effect, from nowhere. The public could believe that Lindbergh and Armstrong had achieved the difficult; it could not believe that Wilbur and Orville had done the impossible.

► Opposite: The first people to witness the Wrights' flights were members of the life-saving crew at Kitty Hawk.
► Above: Early flights at Huffman Prairie near Dayton went largely unnoticed.

Waiting for the story

By 1908, the Wrights were hot news. When Wilbur and Orville returned to Kitty Hawk, reporters cooled their heels waiting to see the wondrous craft in flight.

'I have a wonderful story to tell you.'

The Beekeeper Believed

A mos I. Root was editor of *Gleanings in Bee Culture*, a journal published in Medina, Ohio, for those who kept bees. Actually, Root was interested in everything. Of his editorial purpose, he wrote, "For 32 years, I have been ransacking the world ... and leaving no stone unturned to furnish information of interest and value."

In September 1904, Root hit the mother lode. Following up on a notion that floated in from somewhere, he headed off over 200 miles of unspeakable roads to Huffman Prairie and to brothers Orville and Wilbur. There, he witnessed flight. Actual manned, heavier-than-air flight. At the Wrights' request, the ecstatic editor agreed to embargo his scoop until the first of the year.

Thus, Root's January 1, 1905, issue of *Gleanings* carried the first eyewitness account of flight ever published. "Dear Friends," Root began, "I have a wonderful story to tell you – a story that, in some respects, outrivals the Arabian nights." In a marvelously digressive piece of writing, Root gave a fairly complete account of the Wrights' work to date. With a nice sense of metaphor, he described the Huffman pasture as the place where the Wrights' airplane had " 'learned to fly' ... very much like a young bird just out of its nest learns to practice to use its wings." By chance, Root's visit coincided with the Wrights' first successful flying of a full circle. Of this, the bee man reported:

> *When it turned that circle, and came near the starting-point, I was right in front of it ... (it was) the grandest sight of my life. Imagine a locomotive that has left its track, and is climbing up in the air right toward you – a locomotive without any wheels.... Well, now, imagine that locomotive with wings that spread 20 feet each way, coming right toward you with the tremendous flap of its propellers, and you have something like what I saw.... I tell you friends, the sensation that one feels in such a crisis is something hard to describe.*

► Above: Amos I. Root.

► Opposite: Root's wide-ranging publication describes the 'crisis' of witnessing powered flight.

OUR HOMES, BY A. I. ROOT.

What hath God wrought?—NUM. 23 : 23.

Dear friends, I have a wonderful story to tell you—a story that, in some respects, out-rivals the Arabian Nights fables—a story, too, with a moral that I think many of the younger ones need, and perhaps some of the older ones too if they will heed it. God in his great mercy has permitted me to be, at least somewhat, instrumental in ushering in and introducing to the great wide world an invention that may outrank the electric cars, the automobiles, and all other methods of travel, and one which may fairly take a place beside the telephone and wireless telegraphy. Am I claiming a good deal? Well, I will tell my story, and you shall be the judge. In order to make the story a helpful one I may stop and turn aside a good many times to point a moral.

In our issue for Sept. 1 I told you of two young men, two farmer's boys, who love machinery, down in the central part of Ohio. I am now going to tell you something of two other boys, a *minister's* boys, who love machinery, and who are interested in the modern developments of science and art. Their names are Orville and Wilbur Wright, of Dayton, Ohio. I made mention of them and their work on page 241 of our issue for March 1 last. You may remember it. These two, perhaps by accident, or may be as a matter of taste, began studying the flights of birds and insects. From this they turned their attention to what has been done in the way of enabling men to fly. They not only studied nature, but they procured the best books, and I think I may say all the papers, the world contains on this subject. When I first became acquainted with them, and expressed a wish to read up all there was on the subject, they showed me a library that astonished me; and I soon found they were thoroughly versed, not only in regard to our present knowledge, but every thing that had been done in the past. These boys (they are men now), instead of spending their summer vacation with crowds, and with such crowds as are often questionable, as so many do, went away by themselves to a desert place by the seacoast. You and I have in years past found enjoyment and health in sliding down hill on the snow; but these boys went off to that sandy waste on the Atlantic coast to slide down hill too; but instead of sliding on snow and ice they slid *on air*. With a gliding machine made of sticks and cloth they learned to glide and soar from the top of a hill to the bottom; and by making not only hundreds but *more than a thousand* experiments, they became so proficient in guiding these gliding machines that they could sail like a bird, and control its movements up and down as well as sidewise. Now, this was not altogether for fun or boys' play.* They had a purpose in view. I want to stop right here to draw one of my morals. If I allude to myself somewhat, please do not think I do it because I wish to boast. Some of you have read or heard me tell of the time when my attention was first called to bees. Almost the first thing I did was to go to the bookstores and see what *books* were to be found on the subject. I studied these books day and night, and read them over and over again. Then I procured the books and bee-journals from the old world; and when the language was something I could not manage I hired an interpreter to translate for me until I knew pretty nearly what the book contained. In less than one year I was in touch with the progressive bee-keepers of the world; and the *American Bee Journal*, that had been dropped for lack of support, was started up again. I mention this to show you that my success in bee culture, from the very first, was not luck or chance. It was the result of untiring energy and work. Now let me draw a contrast. During the years that are past, quite a number of men have come to me with their patented hives. A good many of these men had never seen a bee-journal. Some of them who had paid out their hard earnings to the Patent Office had almost never seen a book on bee culture, and they were not sure, from actual experience, of the existence of the queen-bee. We have inventors at the present time who are giving their lives and money to the four winds in the same poor foolish way. If you wish to make a success of any thing, or in any line among the many lines that lie before us in this great world of ours, find out what the great and good men have done in this special line before you.

Well, these two men spent several summers in that wild place, secure from intrusion, with their gliding machine. When they became experts they brought in, as they had planned to do, a gasoline-engine to furnish power, and made a little success with their apparatus before winter set. As soon as the weather would permit, their experiments were resumed the past season. You may have seen something in regard to it in the papers; but as their purpose has been from the beginning to the end to avoid publicity, the great outside world has had but very little opportunity of knowing what is going on. The conditions were so different after applying power that it seemed at first, to a great extent, as if they would have to learn the trade of guiding their little ship all over again. At first they went only a few hundred feet; and as the opportunity for practice in guiding and controlling it was only a few seconds at a time, their progress

---

* When I suggested that, even though sliding down hill on the air was very nice, it must have been quite a task to carry the machine back to the top of the hill every time, the reply was something like this: "Oh! no, Mr. Root—no task at all. Just remember that we always sail *against* the wind; and by a little shifting of the position, the wind does the greater part of the work in carrying it back." It just blows it back (whenever the wind is strong enough) up hill to the starting-point.

Coming around

At Huffman Prairie, Amos Root
witnessed the first circular flight.

The pasture contained a single large tree.

The Helpful Honey Locust

The Wrights flew low at Huffman Prairie, rarely above 30 feet. They did so because their aircraft had a remaining flaw, one they spent much of 1904 and 1905 trying to diagnose. When they flew a circle with the outside wing raised, they had difficulty bringing up the lower inside wing to resume level flight. Sometimes, the aircraft simply continued to circle, unable to right itself. Until the Wrights understood why, they chose to stay near the ground.

The problem was solved by perhaps the only piece of luck the Wright brothers were given. While their field was edged on two sides by trees, the pasture itself contained only a single large tree, a honey locust. In September 1905, Orville was flying when the aircraft started sliding toward the tree, out of control. Instinctively, Orville pointed the airplane down. Immediately, the aircraft accelerated. Immediately, Orville regained control.

Considering this, the Wrights realized that when they flew circles, the inside wing traveled more slowly. Not fast enough, in fact, to avoid a partial stall. From Orville's honey locust experience, they knew that accelerating the craft would overcome stall. Confident now that their machine would not dart dangerously from the skies, they took to higher and longer flights.

On September 26, Wilbur flew 11 miles. On October 3, Orville flew 15. Two days later, Wilbur flew 24. All this flying consisted of lap after three-quarter-mile lap of the Huffman Prairie field: Because the Wrights did not see how they could get the aircraft back to Huffman if they were forced to land elsewhere, they kept within its margins. For longer flights, all the Wrights needed was a more interesting flight path and a larger gas tank.

▶ Opposite and above: The tree in the middle of Huffman Prairie gave the Wrights a hub around which to fly their aircraft.

Onward and upward

By 1910, the Wright Model A – shown here over Huffman Prairie – could carry a pilot and passenger. Wheels were yet to come.

Air traffic

For a time, Huffman Prairie was the world's busiest airport. This 1910 photograph is one of the first to show two Wright Flyers in the air together.

Roaring by

Orville at the controls
of a Wright Model B
training aircraft over
Huffman Prairie.

New technology

The Wrights continued to make flights at Huffman Prairie, even after they became famous. Advancements shown in this 1913 photo include an upright seat for the pilot, the addition of wheels and a radiator.

6

Recognition

<h1 style="text-align:center">The mountain would have to come to them.</h1>

Calling the Government's Bluff

B y October 1905, Wilbur and Orville Wright had a complete aircraft. Out at Huffman Prairie they could launch it, steer it, fly it as long as the fuel held out and land where they wished. The Wrights' aircraft was the greatest new toy ever constructed. The brothers briefly admired their plaything – and then mothballed it. Remarkably, neither Wilbur nor Orville left the ground for the next 30 months – months the brothers used to impose their wills on the U.S. government.

The government was now interested in flight. The government wanted the Wrights to submit their blueprints for review and stage a test flight or two. Then, if the government liked what it saw, it might buy a Wright aircraft.

Wilbur and Orville believed a public demonstration would give the game away. Someone would figure how to duplicate their machine – and threaten their patents. Instead, the brothers suggested that the government set a standard for aircraft – say, a machine able to carry a pilot a stated distance within a set time, and land safely. If a Wright airplane met that standard, the government would be obliged to purchase one.

For two years, neither party moved. The Wrights played their hand, in one phrase, "with the calm confidence of a Christian holding four aces." Octave Chanute worried that some other competitor might sneak in the back door. Wilbur's reply dismissed the competition: "When we see men laboring year after year on points we overcame in a few weeks, without ever getting far enough along to meet the worse points beyond, we know that their rivalry & competition are not to be feared for many years." The Wrights would not budge; the mountain would have to come to them.

▶ Previous page: Elaborate decorations lined the streets of downtown Dayton as the community welcomed the Wrights home from Europe in 1909 with a parade and other festivities.

▶ Above: The brothers meet with a Signal Corps officer to discuss the testing process.

▶ Opposite: Four years after the first flight at Kitty Hawk, the government finally defined what an aircraft should be.

SIGNAL CORPS SPECIFICATION, NO. 486.

ADVERTISEMENT AND SPECIFICATION FOR A HEAVIER-THAN-AIR FLYING MACHINE.

To the Public:

Sealed proposals, in duplicate, will be received at this office until 12 o'clock noon on February 1, 1908, on behalf of the Board of Ordnance and Fortification for furnishing the Signal Corps with a heavier-than-air flying machine. All proposals received will be turned over to the Board of Ordnance and Fortification at its first meeting after February 1 for its official action.

Persons wishing to submit proposals under this specification can obtain the necessary forms and envelopes by application to the Chief Signal Officer, United States Army, War Department, Washington, D. C. The United States reserves the right to reject any and all proposals.

Unless the bidders are also the manufacturers of the flying machine they must state the name and place of the maker.

Preliminary.—This specification covers the construction of a flying machine supported entirely by the dynamic reaction of the atmosphere and having no gas bag.

Acceptance.—The flying machine will be accepted only after a successful trial flight, during which it will comply with all requirements of this specification. No payments on account will be made until after the trial flight and acceptance.

Inspection.—The Government reserves the right to inspect any and all processes of manufacture.

GENERAL REQUIREMENTS.

The general dimensions of the flying machine will be determined by the manufacturer, subject to the following conditions:

1. Bidders must submit with their proposals the following:
   - (a) Drawings to scale showing the general dimensions and shape of the flying machine which they propose to build under this specification.
   - (b) Statement of the speed for which it is designed.
   - (c) Statement of the total surface area of the supporting planes.
   - (d) Statement of the total weight.
   - (e) Description of the engine which will be used for motive power.
   - (f) The material of which the frame, planes, and propellers will be constructed. Plans received will not be shown to other bidders.

2. It is desirable that the flying machine should be designed so that it may be quickly and easily assembled and taken apart and packed for transportation in army wagons. It should be capable of being assembled and put in operating condition in about one hour.

3. The flying machine must be designed to carry two persons having a combined weight of about 350 pounds, also sufficient fuel for a flight of 125 miles.

4. The flying machine should be designed to have a speed of at least forty miles per hour in still air, but bidders must submit quotations in their proposals for cost depending upon the speed attained during the trial flight, according to the following scale:

40 miles per hour, 100 per cent.
39 miles per hour, 90 per cent.
38 miles per hour, 80 per cent.
37 miles per hour, 70 per cent.
36 miles per hour, 60 per cent.
Less than 36 miles per hour rejected.
41 miles per hour, 110 per cent.
42 miles per hour, 120 per cent.
43 miles per hour, 130 per cent.
44 miles per hour, 140 per cent.

5. The speed accomplished during the trial flight will be determined by taking an average of the time over a measured course of more than five miles, against and with the wind. The time will be taken by a flying start, passing the starting point at full speed at both ends of the course. This test subject to such additional details as the Chief Signal Officer of the Army may prescribe at the time.

6. Before acceptance a trial endurance flight will be required of at least one hour during which time the flying machine must remain continuously in the air without landing. It shall return to the starting point and land without any damage that would prevent it immediately starting upon another flight. During this trial flight of one hour it must be steered in all directions without difficulty and at all times under perfect control and equilibrium.

7. Three trials will be allowed for speed as provided for in paragraphs 4 and 5. Three trials for endurance as provided for in paragraph 6, and both tests must be completed within a period of thirty days from the date of delivery. The expense of the tests to be borne by the manufacturer. The place of delivery to the Government and trial flights will be at Fort Myer, Virginia.

8. It should be so designed as to ascend in any country which may be encountered in field service. The starting device must be simple and transportable. It should also land in a field without requiring a specially prepared spot and without damaging its structure.

9. It should be provided with some device to permit of a safe descent in case of an accident to the propelling machinery.

10. It should be sufficiently simple in its construction and operation to permit an intelligent man to become proficient in its use within a reasonable length of time.

11. Bidders must furnish evidence that the Government of the United States has the lawful right to use all patented devices or appurtenances which may be a part of the flying machine, and that the manufacturers of the flying machine are authorized to convey the same to the Government. This refers to the unrestricted right to use the flying machine sold to the Government, but does not contemplate the exclusive purchase of patent rights for duplicating the flying machine.

12. Bidders will be required to furnish with their proposal a certified check amounting to ten per cent of the price stated for the 40-mile speed. Upon making the award for this flying machine these certified checks will be returned to the bidders, and the successful bidder will be required to furnish a bond, according to Army Regulations, of the amount equal to the price stated for the 40-mile speed.

13. The price quoted in proposals must be understood to include the instruction of two men in the handling and operation of this flying machine. No extra charge for this service will be allowed.

14. Bidders must state the time which will be required for delivery after receipt of order.

JAMES ALLEN,
Brigadier General, Chief Signal Officer of the Army.

SIGNAL OFFICE,
WASHINGTON, D. C., *December 23, 1907.*

Speed trials

This photo shows the finish of speed trials at Fort Myer, Virginia, in 1909. The winning award was presented by fellow Daytonian and then-Congressman James M. Cox.

▶ Above: Chanute's triple-wing glider in flight at Kitty Hawk, along with another of Chanute's gliders in action.
▶ Opposite: Octave Chanute with the Wrights at the Kitty Hawk camp.

European interest in powered flight had all but ceased.

Octave Chanute Spills the Beans

O ctave Chanute ran the chat group for aviation. Experimenters worldwide wrote him of their sometimes wildly improbable experiences with flight; Chanute spread the word. And if the word did not wish to be spread, Chanute spread it anyway.

In 1901, European interest in powered flight had all but ceased. Chanute revived it. He revived it by passing along to Europe accounts of the Wrights' breakthrough work. In 1903, Chanute spoke on the Wrights to the Aero-Club de France. A few months later, he supplied scale drawings of the Wrights' 1902 craft. The kindest explanation is that Chanute did not know what he was doing. He did not understand that flight had ceased to be a goal to which many were striving and had become a goal that the Wrights had achieved. And he, Chanute, was passing that solution out to the competition.

French aviators who were Chanute's audience understood matters only somewhat better than Chanute. With more fervor than finesse, they took themselves haltingly to the skies. This renewed activity came during the Wrights' self-imposed grounding.

In France, aviators were with limited success flying aircraft that were knockoffs of the Wrights'. In America, the Wrights – for seemingly obscure reasons – were refusing to fly.

The Wrights' position seemed fishy, or worse. On February 10, 1906, the Paris edition of the *New York Herald* ran an editorial whose title was not likely to sit well with the sons of a bishop of the United Brethren Church. The editorial wondered whether the Wrights were "Fliers or Liars."

Amazement

Once the world caught on to what was happening at Huffman Prairie, fences were needed to keep the crowd back, and a telephone line was installed to get the word out.

The Bishop's boys never joined the circus.

Over the Big Top

The Wrights investigated flight with little thought of how aviation could be turned into a going proposition. In 1907, Wilbur Wright launched a trial balloon: Perhaps he and Orville could make money by giving flying exhibitions. He decided to seek advice from people with experience in such matters.

On March 1, Wilbur wrote to Barnum & Bailey to sound out the circus folk as possible managers of the Wrights' act. Wilbur wrote with a certain lack of show business flair, "We are desirous of getting into communication with parties that would be able to handle that part of the business when the time comes." Nothing came of it, and the Bishop's boys never joined the circus.

▶ Above: The circus came to Dayton, but the Wrights weren't part of it.
▶ Opposite: The closest Orville and Wilbur got to the circus was attending the 1910 International Aviation Tournament in Belmont Park, New York.

Pulling together
Fort Myer, Virginia, 1909.
Soldiers pull a line attached to
a weight-and-pulley system that
was used to help launch Wright
airplanes.

He became a fashion statement.

Europe Discovers Wilbur

I n 1908 Wilbur Wright left for Europe. His airplane followed. He and his brother had finally secured the conditions they wanted for flying, Orville in Virginia, Wilbur in France. In France, Wilbur was at a disadvantage. He was without colleague or companion; he was required to explain what he needed to indifferent French workmen in a language he inexpertly spoke using terms that had no French equivalent. And, most frustratingly, he had to launch himself into the headwinds of the accumulated dismissiveness of French aviation.

On August 8, at an aviation gathering near LeMans, Wilbur took to the skies for a two-minute flight. In that two minutes, he destroyed the pretense of European aviation. Others flew fitfully; Wilbur flew as a great and graceful white bird. In London, *The Times* reported, "All accounts ... attest the complete triumph of the American inventor. The enthusiasm was indescribable."

Wilbur received that peculiarly French form of honor: He became a fashion statement; his distinctive cloth cap appearing everywhere. Europe's nobles and notables crowded around his airstrip. "Princes and millionaires," Wilbur wrote Orville, are "as thick as thieves." Wilbur remained in Europe until year's end, when on December 31 he capped the year with a record flight of two hours, 20 minutes, setting an altitude record of 360 feet.

At first, Orville had equal success – flying demonstration flights for the army at Fort Myer, Virginia. On September 17, however, a propeller blade cracked in flight, the blade flattened and the craft was deprived of thrust. The airplane ducked down. Orville, with Lt. Thomas Selfridge on board, tried to regain control, but crashed at full speed. Selfridge died without regaining consciousness. The accident left Orville with chronic sciatica, one leg shorter than the other, and a limp.

▶ Opposite: A humorous postcard from France, vintage 1908, portrays a caricatured Wilbur making adjustments to a Wright plane.
▶ Above: A year later, both Wilbur and Orville were in France. Here, they confer before one of Wilbur's 1909 flights in Pau. Wilbur's cap set a fashion trend.

Bon chance

Wilbur's trip to Pau, France, to show
off the Flyer was a resounding success.
This 1909 photo shows a rare sight:
Wilbur smiling.

'My God. My God. My God.'

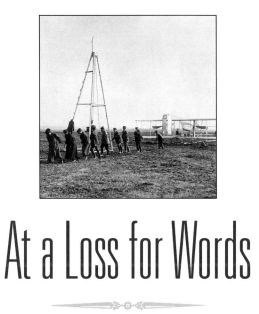

At a Loss for Words

When people saw flight, words failed them. Indeed, the entire English language failed them. There were simply no agreed-upon terms for describing the Wrights' contraption or what it did.

Two men in Dayton saw Wilbur fly, but could not agree on what they had seen. One said that the craft flew "like a duck. She squatted on the ground." The other said, "No, more like a turkey descending from a tree."

One man found expression. In 1909 the Wrights returned to Fort Myer, Virginia, to complete the demonstration flights interrupted by Orville's crash the previous year. The crowd included a well-dressed, elderly gentleman who – having witnessed a palpable, physical thing leave the ground and then return thereto – wandered about saying to no one in particular: "My God. My God. My God."

▶ Above: Preparing to launch the Flyer, Pau, France, 1909.
▶ Opposite: French farmers watch in amazement as the airplane flies at Pau.

An incredible sight

People in Europe and the United States were amazed by the spectacle of Wright flying demonstrations. This one, with Wilbur at the controls, took place on Governor's Island, New York, at the 1909 Hudson-Fulton Exposition. A canoe was attached to the bottom of the plane in case of an emergency water landing. Note the American flag on the front strut.

No power on earth can stop a festival committee whose time has come.

Dayton Claims the Wrights, At Last

The 1908 flights of Orville in Virginia and Wilbur in France made the Wrights world famous; that achieved, their hometown decided it was time to honor the local boys it had previously all but ignored.

Plans were hatched for a Wright Brothers' Home Day Celebration. Wilbur was sour on the idea. Snippily, he wrote to Octave Chanute, "The Dayton presentation has been made the excuse for an elaborate carnival and advertisement of the city under the guise of being an honor to us." Orville, desperately shy, wanted nothing to do with anything so public. Wilbur wrote a tactful letter to the event's sponsors, trying to beg off.

No power on earth, however, can stop a festival committee whose time has come. The event came off on June 17-18, 1909. Wilbur and Orville reviewed parades, shook hands at receptions and listened to concerts. They received medals from representatives of the federal government, the state government and the municipal government. If they found anything objectionable – such as the huge portraits of them, rendered in exploding fireworks – they did not say so.

▶ Above: The Wrights were welcomed back from Europe with great fanfare, and dressed for the occasion.
▶ Opposite: A poster trumpets the homecoming event.

Grand homecoming

Throngs greeted the Wrights at Dayton's Union Station. The celebration that followed lasted two days, June 17-18, 1909.

The community offers praise

The top-hatted Wrights appeared with their father, the Bishop, at the Montgomery County Fairgrounds for speeches and recognition.

Appreciation

The Wright house on Hawthorn Street was festooned with lanterns, flags and bunting for the 1909 celebration.

Proud association

Dayton claimed the Wrights — and so did the Seventh District School.

7

The World

▶ Previous pages: The German military was keenly interested in a 1909 demonstration flight.
▶ Above: Throngs were beginning to gather for the flights over Huffman Prairie.
▶ Opposite: Arthur Welsh, exhibition flier and instructor for the Wrights. He would die in a 1912 crash, while flying a demonstration for the U.S. Army.

From orientation to solo in four hours.

Out of the Bag

By 1911, flight was out of the bag. At Huffman Prairie, fences held back the hundreds who watched students at the Wright flying school practice their takeoffs and landings. Lessons were not cheap – $60 an hour – but student pilots went from orientation to first solo in four hours. The brothers did not teach, but Orville came by often to check on progress. Occasionally, he asked if the students were doing any mushroom hunting. Huffman was a marshy prairie dotted with wild mushrooms. To Orville, the proof that you could handle an aircraft was that you could fly low enough to spot the mushrooms.

The airplanes flown at Huffman were built at the Wright aircraft factory near Third Street and Coleman in West Dayton. The factory reflected its owners. An early employee recalled from his job interview: "While we were carrying on the conversation, (Orville) was going along picking up the brass screws and other small parts that had been brushed off the work benches during the day. They had financed the world's first airplane by the very meager earnings from their bicycle shop and he realized the intrinsic value of those things."

A second said of Wilbur, "He was a brilliant man. He could see through a brick wall. I know sometimes when the motor wouldn't be functioning right, he'd come over and he'd be on this side of the motor and he'd say something over there was wrong. He looked like he was looking through it."

The Wrights had their own ideas on how to run a business. One year, Tom Russell said, they gave each employee a Christmas bonus of "about a pound box of chocolates. Oh boy, we used to laugh at that ... 'Well, now we're sissies.' "

Eyes on the skies

Takeoffs and landings at Huffman Prairie became routine, as did spectators.

'Higher, Orville. Higher.'

The Bishop Ascends

Tom Russell was an NCR machinist who in 1910 applied for work at the Wright Company. Charlie Taylor, who ran the shop, asked Russell if he wore the dust apron common at NCR. Russell said no, he did not; he worried the apron might get snagged if he was working close to a machine. Close to the machine being where Taylor thought a machinist should work, this was the right answer.

Russell was hired. Not long after, Bishop Milton Wright, 81 years old and looking something like God's younger brother, walked into the shop with his face glowing. "He came through the door," Russell said, "and he stopped me and he says, 'Do you know I was up? Orville took me up on a flight today.' And I looked at him. I could hardly believe an old man like that (had flown). He was just tickled to death."

Orville had taken his father for a six-minute ride at Huffman Prairie, ascending to 350 feet. Milton Wright's only comment, made over the clacking of the engine and the whir of the propeller blades, was, "Higher, Orville. Higher."

▶ Opposite: Milton Wright posed for acclaimed Dayton photographer Jane Reece in 1910.
▶ Above: The Bishop catches a nap on the porch of Orville's summer house on Lambert Island in Ontario.

All aboard

Huffman Prairie was the first training ground for powered flight.
This airplane's dual controls
accommodated a student pilot.

Taking care of lawsuits.

In Court, a Lot

The world had resisted the idea of flight. With flight proven, the world could not get enough of it. In 1911, barely two percent of Americans had seen an aircraft in flight; others wanted to, wanted to desperately. And they did not particularly care whether the aviator in question was flying a knockoff machine that infringed upon the Wrights' patents.

Orville cared, largely as a matter of gaining credit where credit was due. Wilbur cared, both for credit and business advantage. He and Orville had made flight possible. There was no reason to treat that as a trivial thing. Wilbur stated: "It is our view that morally the world owes its almost universal use of our system of lateral control (wing warping) to us. It is also our opinion that legally it owes us."

So Wilbur was in court against those who were ripping off his and his brother's patent; he was in court often and determinably and with growing frustration. A Wright employee stated, "Orville was (at the factory) all the time. But then Wilbur was not. Wilbur was in New York, taking care of the lawsuits."

▶ Above: Wilbur dealt with defending the Wrights' patents.
▶ Opposite: The Wrights' key aviation patent. The dotted lines call attention to their glider's wing-warping capability.

No. 821,393.

O. & W. WRIGHT.
FLYING MACHINE.
APPLICATION FILED MAR. 23, 1903.

PATENTED MAY 22, 1906.

3 SHEETS—SHEET 1.

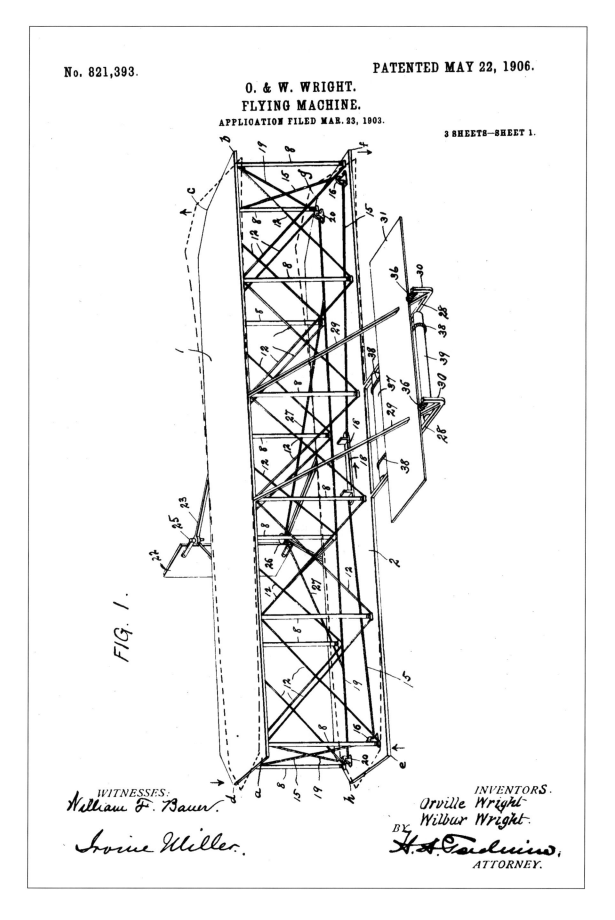

FIG. 1.

WITNESSES:
William F. Bauer.
Irvine Miller.

INVENTORS.
Orville Wright
Wilbur Wright
BY
H. A. Toulmin,
ATTORNEY.

225

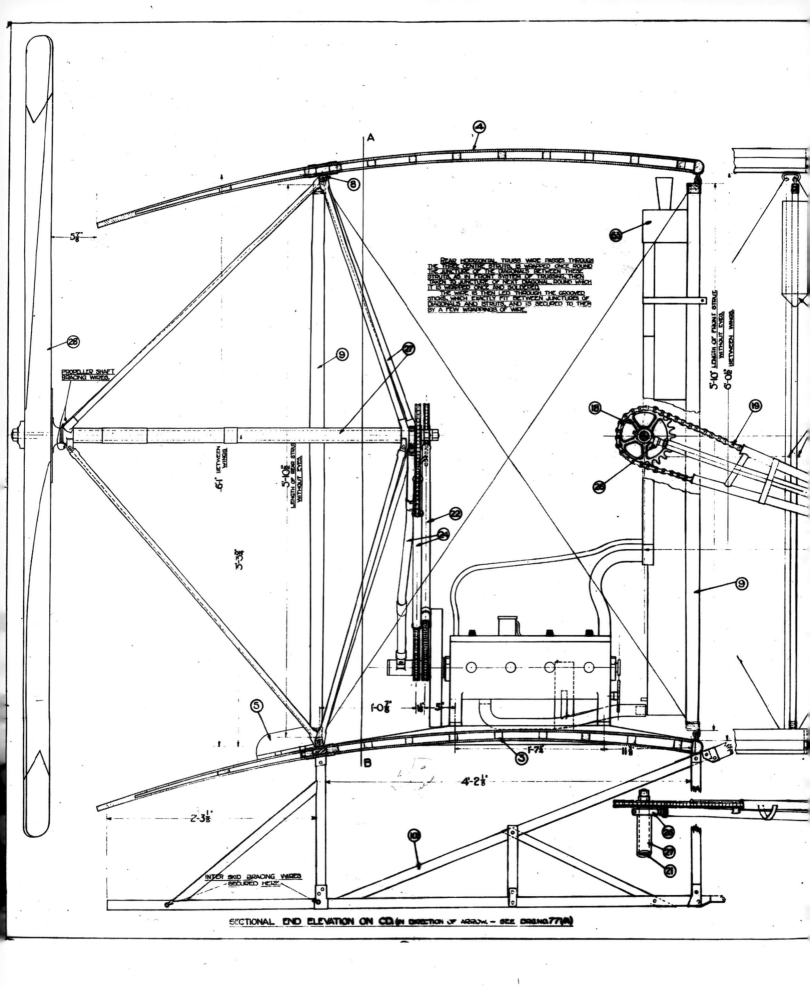

SECTIONAL END ELEVATION ON CD (IN DIRECTION OF ARROW - SEE DRG.NO.77(A))

Moving parts

This line drawing, rendered by the Science Museum
in London, England, shows the first aircraft transmission
system for the 1903 Wright Flyer.

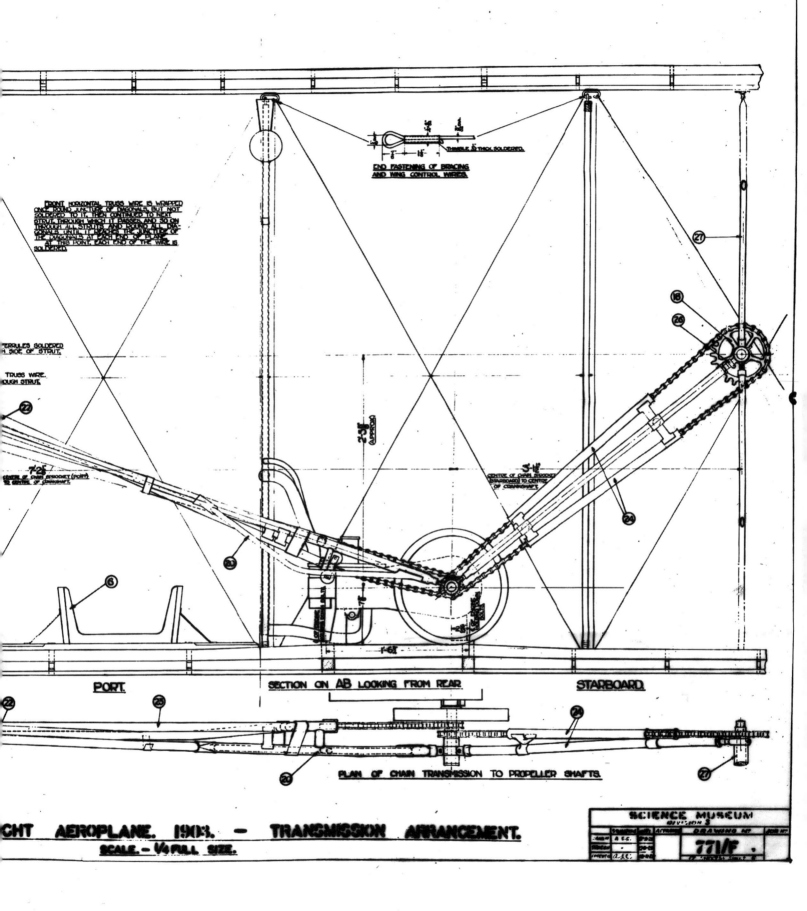

END FASTENING OF BRACING AND WING CONTROL WIRES.

THIMBLE ⅜ THICK. SOLDERED.

FRONT HORIZONTAL TRUSS WIRE IS WRAPPED ONCE ROUND JUNCTION OF DIAGONALS, BUT NOT SOLDERED TO IT, THEN CONTINUED TO NEXT STRUT, THROUGH WHICH IT PASSES, AND SO ON THROUGH ALL STRUTS, AND ROUND ALL DIAGONALS UNTIL IT REACHES THE CENTRE OF THE DIAGONALS AT EACH END OF PLANE. AT THIS POINT, EACH END OF THE WIRE IS SOLDERED.

FERRULES SOLDERED EACH SIDE OF STRUT.

TRUSS WIRE. THROUGH STRUT.

CENTRE OF CHAIN SPROCKET (PORT) TO CENTRE OF CRANKSHAFT.

CENTRE OF CHAIN SPROCKET (STARBOARD) TO CENTRE OF CRANKSHAFT.

PORT.

SECTION ON AB LOOKING FROM REAR.

STARBOARD.

PLAN OF CHAIN TRANSMISSION TO PROPELLER SHAFTS.

WRIGHT AEROPLANE. 1903. — TRANSMISSION ARRANGEMENT.
SCALE. — ¼ FULL SIZE.

SCIENCE MUSEUM
DIVISION 3

DRAWING Nº
771/F.

▶ Above: Orville and Wilbur in Pau, France, 1909.
▶ Opposite: Wilbur, in the December 17, 1903, photograph showing the first powered flight.

A Team No Longer

O n May 2, 1912, Wilbur Wright returned from Boston, indisposed. Several days later he took to his bed. Bishop Wright's diary for May 8 reads: "There seems to be a sort of typhoidal fever prevailing. It usually lasts about a week." Speculation was that Wilbur contracted typhoid in Boston from contaminated shellfish.

Life went on. On May 10, Bishop Wright and son Lorin sallied forth to watch the Ringling circus parade; the Bishop counted a dozen camels, 20 or so elephants and a steam whistle. Two days later, NCR President John H. Patterson paid a sick call on Wilbur. Doctors came; nurses stayed. On May 15, former President Teddy Roosevelt, a candidate in the pending Ohio presidential primary, spoke in Dayton. Orville went, but the crowds were too great. Instead, he listened to a suffragette.

Three days later, Wilbur lost consciousness. Katharine wrote Reuchlin, living in Kansas, to return home. The Bishop was optimistic. His diary for May 24 reads, "Wilbur seems, in nearly every respect, better." The Bishop's eyes deceived him; perhaps he wished them to. Wilbur died early on May 30, aged 45.

His passing drew 25,000 to Dayton's First Presbyterian Church and eulogies from around the world. None was more apt, though, than the words Bishop Wright wrote in his diary the day of his son's death: "A short life, full of consequences. An unfailing intellect, imperturbable temper, great self-reliance and as great modesty, seeing the right clearly, pursuing it steadfastly, he lived and died."

Wilbur had several months earlier provided a sort of epitaph for himself. In a letter to Octave Chanute, he wrote:

> *If there be a domineering, tyrant thought, it is the conception that the problem of flight may be solved by man. When once this idea has invaded the brain, it possesses it exclusively. It is then a haunting thought, a walking nightmare, impossible to cast off. If we now consider the pitying contempt with which such a line of research is appreciated, we may somewhat conceive the unhappy lot of the investigator whose soul is thus possessed.*

Paying their respects
Some 25,000 people gathered around the First Presbyterian Church in downtown Dayton for Wilbur Wright's funeral in 1912.

They were left behind.

The World They Made

A s Milton Wright wrote, Wilbur's life was "full of consequence." Yet, while Wilbur was mourned, the field of aviation itself did not suffer much by his early death. In 1908, the Wrights stood alone, honored and unchallenged. In the next four years – the final four of Wilbur's life – they were left behind, as aviators in Europe and America mastered what they had to teach and soon outdistanced them. By 1912, the Wrights no longer held a single world record.

The Wrights had solved the question of flight without giving much thought to its future. Orville once said he had never expected things to develop as far as they had – and he said this in 1917, aviation's early history. Events override expectations. In 1909, the French Peace Society gave its annual medal to Wilbur and Orville. They had, the society said, made war impossible. Successful invasion depended on surprise. With aircraft overhead to scope out an enemy's maneuvers, surprise was no longer possible. And, without the advantage of surprise, war would cease. Actually not. Wilbur flew through the French sky in 1908; in 1915, his place was taken by Baron von Richtofen.

The question of what Orville and Wilbur's work meant begs the question of what would have happened if they hadn't done it. Pure speculation, but it is hard to imagine anyone else creating even a Kitty Hawk-quality aircraft prior to 1915. Given that, aircraft technology might well not have undergone the pressure-cooker of development of the First World War. Given that, it is hard to see the Luftwaffe over London, Japanese Zeroes over Pearl Harbor or a single American bomber over Hiroshima.

Be that as it may. Wilbur died young and, in light of what would come, innocent. Orville survived to see much of what the world made of their invention: Lindbergh crossing the Atlantic in 1927. Airmail service across the Pacific in 1934. Regular trans-Atlantic passenger service in 1939. The first jet aircraft – German fighters – in 1944.

For all these, Orville was a spectator. In part, the reason was the painful sciatica that traced to his 1908 crash. Often, the pain was such that he could barely rise from a chair. As the vibration of flight exacerbated his condition, Orville Wright did not like to fly.

▶ Opposite: A B-29 bomber from World War II.
▶ Above: Claude Grahame-White's 1910 flight over Washington, D.C., ended with the first airplane landing in the city, on Executive Avenue. On the left is the Old Executive Office Building.

The old meets the new

In 1912, a Wright airplane made a demonstration flight in London, including a pass through Tower Bridge.

Orville, to his depths, felt betrayed.

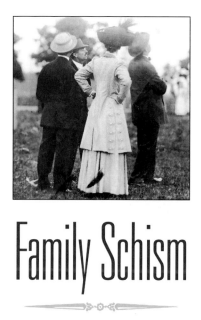

Family Schism

Wilbur and Orville had been raised in an extraordinarily close family. Family, Milton Wright taught, and family alone was the sole earthly thing upon which one could depend.

After Wilbur's death in 1912, Milton, Orville and Katharine Wright moved into Hawthorn Hill, the Oakwood mansion that was the one extravagance of Orville's life. They intended, Orville believed, to live out their lives together. Brother Reuchlin lived out his own life in self-imposed exile in Kansas; brother Lorin – upon whose four children Orville doted – had a family of his own in Dayton.

After the death of Bishop Milton Wright, aged 88, in 1917, family for Orville was Katharine, and Katharine alone. In mid-1926, Katharine Wright – aged 52 – announced that she was engaged to Henry J. Haskell, a fellow trustee of Oberlin College. And Orville, to his depths, felt betrayed. Katharine had betrayed the family, he thought, a betrayal not lessened by the fact that the courtship had gone on for a year and not a word to him. Henry and Katharine married and moved to Kansas City, where he became editor and part owner of the *Kansas City Star.*

They left Dayton without a word from Orville, who swore he would never speak to his sister again. He carried that intention almost to her grave. In early 1929, Katharine contracted pneumonia. Only the entreaties of Lorin prompted him to travel to Kansas City before she died.

▶ Opposite: Members of the Wright family, in 1910 and happier times, watch an aircraft in flight.

▶ Above: After Katharine's announced engagement, Orville swore he would never speak to her again. He relented when she was on her deathbed. This photo was taken in the early 1920s.

Mansion on the hill

Hawthorn Hill, Orville's Oakwood
estate, and his only extravagance.

He survived Wilbur quietly.

Orville Alone

O rville Wright died of a heart attack on January 30, 1948, at the age of 76. He had survived Wilbur by a third of a century. He did so quietly.

He was one of the famous people of the world, a fact he tried to get others to ignore, in part by ignoring it himself. In 1916, aged 45, he sold his interest in the Wright Company. He puttered in a laboratory he kept on Dayton's North Broadway Street, not accomplishing much, and spent time at his cabin at Georgian Bay, an extension of Lake Huron in Ontario.

With nieces and nephews he was patient and playful; with others he remained reticent. He did not explain himself. James Wilbur Jacobs, the son of a long-time Wright workman, said, "I never recall Orville speaking of his brother Wilbur." Another employee, Ernest Dubel, stated, "I never heard him talk of Kitty Hawk."

An interviewer asked Orville's niece, Ivonette Wright Miller, if her uncle ever explained why he had wanted to fly. Ivonette replied, "No."

Orville's shyness excluded most others, almost excluding the President of the United States. Once Franklin Roosevelt came to Dayton, campaigning for re-election. Former Ohio Governor James Cox, a Dayton resident, invited Orville to lunch with the President. It was a request Orville could hardly refuse. Later – and unexpectedly – Orville found himself riding between Roosevelt and Cox in an open touring car, an abductee of the Roosevelt campaign. When the car temporarily stopped in Orville's Oakwood neighborhood, he climbed out, thanked the President for lunch, and walked home.

▶ Opposite: Orville, at Huffman Prairie, in 1916. The airplane has an automatic pilot mechanism.

▶ Above: One of the last portraits of Orville Wright.

241

Historic company

During a presidential visit in 1940, Orville found himself sandwiched between Franklin D. Roosevelt and former Ohio governor and *Dayton Daily News* publisher James M. Cox in the back seat of Roosevelt's car.

New York debut

In 1909, Wilbur made a series of flights from Governor's Island in New York City for the Aeronautics Committee of the Hudson-Fulton Commission. They were the first airplane flights in the city. Wilbur was paid $15,000.

Fine-tuning

Orville makes adjustments to a new generation of airplane, the 1910 Model B, at Huffman Prairie. The plane now had bicycle-style wheels to supplement its runners.

Germany, 1909

One of the many demonstration flights that brought the Wrights fame in Europe.

Reaching for speed

Wilbur and Orville with Ralph Johnstone and the Wrights' "Baby Grand" racing plane in Belmont Park, New York, 1910. Johnstone was one of the many early pilots to die in flying accidents.

Left behind

This photograph taken in 1908 showed the remnants of the Wrights' 1903 camp at Kitty Hawk – and the 1902 glider – in weathered ruins.

Sources

Books

▶ Mark Bernstein, *Grand Eccentrics*, Orange-Frazer Press, 1996.

▶ James E. Cox, *Journey Through My Years*, Simon & Schuster, 1946.

▶ Tom Crouch, *The Bishop's Boys*, W.W. Norton, 1989.

▶ C. H. Gibbs-Smith, *The Invention of the Airplane*, Taplinger, 1966.

▶ Clive Hart, *The Prehistory of Flight*, University of California Press, 1985.

▶ Peter L. Jakab, *Visions of a Flying Machine*, Smithsonian Institution Press, 1990

▶ Fred C. Kelly, *The Wright Brothers*, Harcourt, Brace & Company, 1943.

▶ Walter Lord, *The Good Years*, Harper & Row, 1960.

▶ Marvin W. McFarland, editor (two volumes), *The Papers of Wilbur and Orville Wright*, McGraw-Hill, 1953.

▶ Bishop Milton Wright, *Diaries: 1857-1917*, Wright State University, 1999.

▶ Robert H. Wiebe, *The Search for Order – 1877-1920*, Hill and Wang, 1967.

▶ Orville Wright, *How We Invented the Airplane*, David McKay Company, Inc., 1953.

Other

▶ *The Criterion*, March 1905.

▶ *Gleanings in Bee Culture*, January 1, 1905.

▶ *Evening Item*, published by Wilbur and Orville Wright, May-July 1890, Dayton Collection, Dayton and Montgomery County (Ohio) Public Library.

▶ Irwin Feller, "The Urban Location of United States Invention, 1860-1910," *Explorations in Economic History*, Spring 1971.

▶ Minutes Book, Annual Club of the Ten Dayton Boys, Dayton Collection, Dayton and Montgomery County (Ohio) Public Library.

▶ Official Program, The Wright Brothers Home Celebration, Dayton, Ohio, June 17-18.

▶ Wright Brothers Oral History Project, University of Dayton, 1967.

▶ Arthur Ruhl, "History of Kill Devil Hill," *Colliers*, May 30, 1908.

▶ Wilbur Wright, "An Evening Tour to Miamisburg," account of bicycle trip excerpted from a letter to Katharine Wright, September 18, 1892

▶ Interviews by author, including Ivonette Wright Miller and Wilkinson Wright.

Photography

Wright State University

▶ Special Collections and Archives, Wright State University Libraries. Many of the photographs in this book came from the Wright Brothers Collection in the Special Collections and Archives. Special Collections and Archives administers collections in both the Paul Laurence Dunbar Library and the Fordham Health Sciences Library. The Dunbar Library's emphasis on aviation history and the Fordham Library's emphasis on aerospace medicine and human factors engineering combine to make Wright State a nationally known repository for the documentation of some of the 20th century's most dramatic technologies. The other major focus for both libraries is the local and regional history of the Miami Valley area of Ohio. Together, the libraries offer a comprehensive historical perspective on the region, aviation and aerospace medicine. Photos from Wright State University's Special Collections and Archives appear on pages: 11, 12, 19, 20, 21 (2), 22-23, 25, 26-27, 28 (2), 29, 30-31, 32, 33, 34-35, 36, 37, 40, 41, 42-43, 44 (top left), 59, 60, 61, 64, 68, 70-71, 72, 73, 74-75, 76-77, 78-79, 80-81, 83, 84, 85, 86-87, 88, 89, 92, 93, 94-95, 96-97, 98-99, 100-101, 102-103, 107, 110, 111, 112-113, 114, 115, 116-117, 122, 123, 124-125, 127, 128-129, 130, 131, 134, 135, 136-137, 138, 139, 140-141, 142-143, 144-145, 146-147, 148-149, 158-159, 160, 161, 162-163, 164, 165, 166-167, 168, 169, 173, 184, 186-187, 188 (3), 189, 193, 194-195, 196, 197, 198-199, 200, 201, 202-203, 206-207, 208-209, 210-211, 212-213, 215, 220, 221, 224, 228, 229, 233, 234-235, 240-241, 242-243, 244-245, 248-249, 250-251, 252-253.

William Mayfield

▶ The Marvin Christian Collection, Photos by William Mayfield. William Mayfield launched his career as a photographer in 1909. A year later, with Orville Wright at the controls of the Wright Flyer, Mayfield made one of the first photographs from an airplane, of the Wright hangar at Huffman Prairie. He continued to fly at every opportunity, and met and photographed many pioneers of aviation. Aerial photography remained a passion throughout his 60-year career. Mayfield photos appear on pages: 13, 14, 15, 16-17, 24, 38-39, 44 (top center), 46-47, 48-49, 50-51, 52-53, 54-55, 56-57, 62-63, 65, 66-67, 69, 90-91, 105, 108-109, 118, 119, 120-121, 126, 132-133, 151, 153, 156, 157, 170-171, 172, 174-175, 176-177, 178-179, 180-181, 183, 185, 190-191, 192, 204, 205, 216, 217, 218-219, 222-223, 225, 226-227, 230-231, 232, 236, 237, 238-239, 246-247.

Dayton Daily News

▶ The *Dayton Daily News* Reference Library. *Dayton Daily News* photos appear on pages: 44 (top right and bottom), 45, 50-51, 56-57, 62-63, 106, 152, 154-155, 242-243.